Your Secret Personality

Discover The Surprisingly Simple Truth Behind Your Personality And Enjoy A Better Life

Alan Fensin

You can get free extra answer sheets for the personality test at the website www.yoursecretpersonality.com

Copyright © 2017 by Alan Fensin
All rights reserved

No part of this book may be reproduced or
transmitted in any form or by any means,
electronic or mechanical, including
photocopying, recording or by any
information storage and retrieval system
without written permission from the author,
except for the inclusion of brief quotations in
a review.

Printed in the United States of America
Published in 2017 by
Burlington Book Division of Burlington
National Inc.

ISBN: 1-57706-655-3
ISBN: 978-1-57706-655-2

Contents

Chapter Five:

Introduction

He who knows others is learned. He who knows himself is wise. - Lao Tzu

What if you could read a book, take a test, and recognize the strengths and weakness of your personality? What if that book then taught you how to improve and enhance your life? And what if it is something that is easy to understand and makes perfect sense? That something is whole mind thinking, and *Your Secret Personality* will show you how to do it.

In order to grow in positive ways, we first have to know ourselves. *Your Secret Personality* presents a journey intended to increase your ability to understanding hidden secrets within yourself. It can become a powerful tool for healing and transformation.

The only way growth can truly take place is through your own efforts. Understanding yourself is the bridge to creating a new, richer world, both inside of you and in the world around you.

In his book, *Motivation and Personality*, Abraham Maslow categorizes human needs into seven levels, known as Maslow's Need Hierarchy. The seven levels encompass physiological needs such as food and shelter; needs for security; sex; love, and acceptance; the need for worth and esteem; and finally, the need for knowledge about life. Therefore, to achieve wholeness, we must satisfy our highest needs, including self-knowledge.

Most of us bounce through life haphazardly, guided by our likes and dislikes and our old familiar patterns. We are influenced by advertisements and by our friends in our individual choices of habits and activities. What if we could use self-knowledge to move beyond everyday life and into our fuller development?

Different personalities achieve best results with different individual advice. A simple example is that an overly serious individual needs to lighten up; conversely, an overly–playful individual needs to become more serious. What differentiates this book from most other psychology books is the extensive emphasis on how each of the different personalities can grow towards a happier and more centered individual.

Your Secret Personality offers general yet comprehensive information about the many elements of your psychological life. By studying your personality, you can determine which changes will be most effective for you. By using the instructions in this book, you can transform your life and be happier and more fulfilled.

The personality system described herein will dramatically advance your self-observation. It allows you to achieve a spectacular breakthrough in your self–understanding. It's also a very accessible psychological model that most people can easily understand. It will provide an opening in your life that can lead to a deepening of wisdom. Then you can more easily experience the full 360 degree spectrum of possibilities and world views.

Before birth, we each felt safe and secure in our mother's womb without worry or anxiety. Very early during the first year of our lives, we began to feel separate and lose our total trust in life. We began to experience various needs and desires that were no longer always fulfilled.

In the quest to satisfy those needs, we learned to modify our natural behavior with changes that we thought would bring the fulfillment of our needs. These behavior modifications are normal and essential in helping us survive childhood. Still, with time, our identification with this modified behavior becomes so strong that we identify with this learned behavior and forget our true self.

As adults, our childhood choices now determine our automatic responses. Our attention is controlled by an unending succession of desires, emotions and fears that keep us from knowing our true self. An important part of psychological growth is recognizing and understanding these automatic responses, which are the very things that keeps us from growth. This will turn our negative traits into gifts so that we become better-adjusted, happier people.

Understanding our true selves allows recognition of other objective measures for truth beyond our own individual perception of how things are. Once we realize that there are other equally valid ways of seeing things, it opens up a new tolerance in our dealing with the rest of humanity and allows us to solve relationship problems.

Great people usually have one thing in common – a deep knowledge of themselves.

There are an infinite number of different and distinct personalities, just as there are an infinite number of points on a circle. However, we can divide the circle of a compass into North, South, East and West, and we can similarly divide the infinite number of unique personalities into basic directions or chief personality features.

It is not our intent to force the reader to choose only one personality type from the several offered. People are not purely one personality style and usually have traits of many personality types. Still, for each of us, there is generally one personality type that predominates.

Due to the nature of this book, both positive and negative aspects of each personality are examined; however, this book is not intended to pass judgment on anyone. Each personality has different strengths and weaknesses, but in the final analysis there is no personality that is any better than any other. There are, however, different basic types of personalities.

Most people also praise this book because of the insights it gives them about other people. The world looks very different to each of the different personalities, and by understanding the way others feel, you can move out of your limiting reality and understand them better. You'll be amazed at what you can learn about yourself, your friends and your family.

Chapter One: Three Brains

Three Centers

This exploration of your secret personality has been handed down through many generations. It is part of an ancient method of looking deeply into the human personality.

The personality system in this book has very ancient origins. No one is sure exactly when or where the three brains concept originated. It may have been in Babylon about twenty-five hundred years ago or elsewhere in the Middle East. According to ancient science, one or two forces are not enough and a third force must be present to produce a phenomenon.

The Essenes and the very early Christian mystics used a similar but much simplified system. The earliest written records on this subject are the writings of Evagrius Ponticus, a Greek Christian living in the Middle East about 300 years after Christ.

Some of the aspects of this ancient wisdom were passed down through a mystic named George Ivanovich Gurdjieff (1866 - 1949). He taught a personality typing system that came from various sources, including ancient Christianity. He taught that three types of individual personalities came from the three distinct behaviors of the human brains. Only in the twentieth century has this work become familiar to people in the Western world.

Paul MacLean (1913 - 2007), a neuroscientist at Yale Medical and the National Institutes of Health, made significant contributions with his triune brain model.

Modern science has added to this knowledge and found that the human brain is physically made up of three separate but very interconnected brains.

The oldest and most critical part of the brain is for survival and is named the basal ganglia. For simplicity, it is often called the reptilian brain or the instinctive brain. It is located at the top of the brain stem and continuing downward to form the spinal cord.

This instinctive brain controls the body's vital functions, such as heart rate, breathing, body temperature and all the basics that keep us alive and safe from our enemies. It works quickly, simply and takes care of the basics. It is where our subconscious resides, and even when we are asleep it is awake and makes sure our body functions properly. Because of its flight, fight or freeze control, it is the *anger center* of our personality.

Our second brain is called the Limbic System or midbrain. It grew over our old brain and is responsible for the emotions that make us who we are. It also takes care of our memory and other aspects of learning. It is in charge of imagery, video and music enjoyment. All mammals have a well-developed second brain. It is the memory, relationship and *emotional center* of our personality. In our social lives, emotions are a key driver in our decision making.

Our third brain is called the neocortex (Latin for *new tree bark growth*). It is well developed in the higher mammals such as humans and the higher primates such as apes and dolphins. It is the logical center responsible for planning, abstractions, language and logic. It is the part of the brain that allowed humans to build a rocket ship, land men on the Moon and make I-phones. Because it can logically evaluate most of the dangers of the world it is called *fear center* of our personality.

All three of your brains are extremely well interconnected, communicate with each other, and form a complete personality. None of the centers or specialized locations works in a vacuum without input from the other parts of the brain. Instead, they work as part of a whole system that includes many parts of the brain.

However, for each individual, one of these three brains is usually more powerful than the other two, and that establishes the foundation of who you are. When you realize which part of your brain has the most control of your personality, you will learn a lot about yourself. You will also learn how to become more than yourself and become the person you were meant to be.

Three Personality Centers

A human being is a part of the whole called by us universe. A part limited in time and space. He experiences himself, his thoughts and feelings as something separate from the rest – a kind of optical delusion of his consciousness. This delusion is a kind of prison for us. Our task must be to free ourselves from this prison. – Albert Einstein

Since this hundreds of years old personality typing method has been around so long, isn't it out of date by now?

Not any more than the human personality is. Over the ages, we humans have transformed the world around us but have remained psychologically unchanged. We are physically bigger and healthier, and we live several times as long as we once did. But we are no smarter and no more complex than we were more than three thousand years ago.

So far as our personalities are concerned, we have not changed at all over that long period. We know this from the writings of the ancient Greeks and Chinese. If Ulysses or an emperor of ancient China were able to time-travel to America today, he would certainly be amazed by our technology and perhaps by our life-style. But he would not be amazed by our personalities. It would be the same old thing. He'd have met people like us before.

Just as humans have three brains, they also have three distinct basic personalities. There are billions of humans and billions of personalities. However, most people develop one of the three distinct thought patterns we have come to call personality. And these three personalities correspond to the three brains.

The *instinctive brain* is also called the *anger center*. It is responsible for self-preservation. The instinctive brain is symbolically the *human gut* since people who belong to it tend to act from gut instincts. They are more spontaneous in their instinctive or intuitive reactions than the other groups. Anger is a frequent issue in their relationships. Their anger may be either cold or hot. Or their behavior may even indicate a denial of anger.

The *emotional brain* is also called the *feeling center* or symbolically the *human heart* because this group is more emotional and more concerned with feelings than those who belong to the other two groups. This brain is responsible for our emotional features as well as memory and some facets of learning.

The logical brain is associated with functions such as language, abstraction and planning. The *logical brain* is also called the *fear center* or the symbolical *human head* because this group is most comfortable as rational thinkers. Since coping with the world is a major concern, they use logic to try to make sense of reality. The head group is often seen by some as objective and impersonal. Ironically, much of their thinking can be about personal relationships.

Some people know which of the three centers, anger center, emotional center, or fear center, is their dominant center. But most people are not sure, and this book will assist you in identifying yourself.

Your brain is literally making many millions of new connections ever single minute of the day. This brain rewiring is how your personality developed and how you can change for the better. Therefore, it is possible to awaken your brain to your strongest self. Chapter five of this book gives insights to train your brain and break free of your self-sabotage and inner conflicts.

14   Your Secret Personality

Chapter Two: Your Secret Personality Test

This Chapter has the personality test. There are nine tests with ten questions each. Read the statements on the next page and determine your level of agreement with each statement. Circle the number on the scale which best describes you on the following page. Ten represents your greatest agreement with the statement and one represents your least agreement. You should record your reaction quickly and without prolonged examination.

Many people do not want to take a personality test. If you do not like tests or if you just want to save time, you can skip these tests and go directly to "Nine Personalities" on page 36 and continue reading through "Chapter Three The Personality Types" on page 43. That chapter has four pages on each of the nine personalities and most people can determine their personality just by reading the four page descriptions. Most people can determine their personality by reading about them instead of taking a test.

As people reach adulthood, their core personality is sometimes masked by growth or the necessities of life. Therefore if you are in doubt about answering any question choose the answer that best describes you when you were (or if you are now) under the age of 23.

If you prefer not to mark up this book, you can get a free download of the answer sheets at the website. www.yoursecretpersonality.com where all nine answer sheets can be downloaded in one PDF file for an easy printout.

Read the statements below and determine your level of agreement with each statement. Circle the number on the scale which describes you on the next page.

Ten represents your greatest agreement with the statement and one represents your least agreement. You should record your reaction quickly and without prolonged examination.

TEST A

1.	I often impress others as a being a perfectionist.
2.	I usually have a cold anger rather than the kind that boils over.
3.	I like others to see me as highly principled.
4.	I am aware of the imperfections of life and often want to correct them.
5.	I don't like being critical, yet I do notice when things are wrong.
6.	I know that sometimes I am too judgmental and impatient.
7.	I am earnest and self-disciplined.
8.	I don't like losing control of myself.
9.	I am direct, formal and idealistic.
10.	In difficult situations I know where I stand.

SCORE SHEET A

1.	1	2	3	4	5	6	7	8	9	10
	least agreement							most agreement		
2.	1	2	3	4	5	6	7	8	9	10
	least agreement							most agreement		
3.	1	2	3	4	5	6	7	8	9	10
	least agreement							most agreement		
4	1	2	3	4	5	6	7	8	9	10
	least agreement							most agreement		
5.	1	2	3	4	5	6	7	8	9	10
	least agreement							most agreement		
6.	1	2	3	4	5	6	7	8	9	10
	least agreement							most agreement		
7.	1	2	3	4	5	6	7	8	9	10
	least agreement							most agreement		
8.	1	2	3	4	5	6	7	8	9	10
	least agreement							most agreement		
9.	1	2	3	4	5	6	7	8	9	10
	least agreement							most agreement		
10.	1	2	3	4	5	6	7	8	9	10
	least agreement							most agreement		

Total your score for the circled numbers for these last ten questions here: _____

Read the statements below and determine your level of agreement with each statement. Circle the number on the scale which describes you on the next page.

Ten represents your greatest agreement with the statement and one represents your least agreement. You should record your reaction quickly and without prolonged examination.

TEST B

1. People often think of me as a leader.
2. I am a self-confident and powerful person.
3. I usually do not respect people who are weak, but I do respect those who stand up to me.
4. I am loyal to my family and friends and might fight to protect them.
5. On occasion, I can become loud or insulting. I don't always care if people like me as long as they respect me.
6. I sometimes see the world as a hostile place that needs to be conquered.
7. I do not let people take advantage of me and, if they do, I can seek revenge.
8. I can take charge of many situations and inspire courage and strength in others.
9. I can champion others and use my resources to help them make something of themselves.
10. Life can be a struggle, but with courage you can do great things.

SCORE SHEET B

1.	1	2	3	4	5	6	7	8	9	10
	least agreement							most agreement		
2.	1	2	3	4	5	6	7	8	9	10
	least agreement							most agreement		
3.	1	2	3	4	5	6	7	8	9	10
	least agreement							most agreement		
4	1	2	3	4	5	6	7	8	9	10
	least agreement							most agreement		
5.	1	2	3	4	5	6	7	8	9	10
	least agreement							most agreement		
6.	1	2	3	4	5	6	7	8	9	10
	least agreement							most agreement		
7.	1	2	3	4	5	6	7	8	9	10
	least agreement							most agreement		
8.	1	2	3	4	5	6	7	8	9	10
	least agreement							most agreement		
9.	1	2	3	4	5	6	7	8	9	10
	least agreement							most agreement		
10.	1	2	3	4	5	6	7	8	9	10
	least agreement							most agreement		

Total your score for the circled numbers for these last ten questions here: _____

Read the statements below and determine your level of agreement with each statement. Circle the number on the scale which describes you on the next page.

Ten represents your greatest agreement with the statement and one represents your least agreement. You should record your reaction quickly and without prolonged examination.

TEST C

1	I impress others as being a peaceful person.
2.	I am easy-going and comfortable, and I usually avoid things that can cause anxiety.
3.	I do not like to live with a lot of disharmony or conflict in my life.
4.	I sometimes have difficulty in getting really motivated.
5.	I shift gears slowly when moving from task to task and once I do, I tend to remain pointed toward the new task.
6.	With my soothing, gentle way, I often help others relax.
7.	I can be supportive and generous with my family and friends.
8.	I am usually very diplomatic but can sometimes be very honest, and this can sometimes offend others.
9.	I am a peacemaker and don't seek retribution or vengeance.
10.	I usually understand both sides of a conflict.

SCORE SHEET C

1.	1	2	3	4	5	6	7	8	9	10
	least agreement							most agreement		
2.	1	2	3	4	5	6	7	8	9	10
	least agreement							most agreement		
3.	1	2	3	4	5	6	7	8	9	10
	least agreement							most agreement		
4	1	2	3	4	5	6	7	8	9	10
	least agreement							most agreement		
5.	1	2	3	4	5	6	7	8	9	10
	least agreement							most agreement		
6.	1	2	3	4	5	6	7	8	9	10
	least agreement							most agreement		
7.	1	2	3	4	5	6	7	8	9	10
	least agreement							most agreement		
8.	1	2	3	4	5	6	7	8	9	10
	least agreement							most agreement		
9.	1	2	3	4	5	6	7	8	9	10
	least agreement							most agreement		
10.	1	2	3	4	5	6	7	8	9	10
	least agreement							most agreement		

Total your score for the circled numbers for these last ten questions here: _____

Read the statements below and determine your level of agreement with each statement. Circle the number on the scale which describes you on the next page.

Ten represents your greatest agreement with the statement and one represents your least agreement. You should record your reaction quickly and without prolonged examination.

TEST D

1.	I usually listen to others with concern and empathy.
2.	I don't have a lot of personal needs.
3.	I like being needed others and being able to help them.
4.	I like to be loved and needed by others.
5.	I am more likely to flatter someone than criticize them.
6.	In relationships, I typically take care of others more than thay take care of me.
7.	I notice that many people depend on me.
8.	I prefer helping people in a one-to one relationship.
9.	I am sympathetic and feel good about people depending on me.
10.	I strive to advise and care for my friends.

SCORE SHEET D

1.	1	2	3	4	5	6	7	8	9	10
	least agreement							most agreement		
2.	1	2	3	4	5	6	7	8	9	10
	least agreement							most agreement		
3.	1	2	3	4	5	6	7	8	9	10
	least agreement							most agreement		
4	1	2	3	4	5	6	7	8	9	10
	least agreement							most agreement		
5.	1	2	3	4	5	6	7	8	9	10
	least agreement							most agreement		
6.	1	2	3	4	5	6	7	8	9	10
	least agreement							most agreement		
7.	1	2	3	4	5	6	7	8	9	10
	least agreement							most agreement		
8.	1	2	3	4	5	6	7	8	9	10
	least agreement							most agreement		
9.	1	2	3	4	5	6	7	8	9	10
	least agreement							most agreement		
10.	1	2	3	4	5	6	7	8	9	10
	least agreement							most agreement		

Total your score for the circled numbers for these last ten questions here: _____

Read the statements below and determine your level of agreement with each statement. Circle the number on the scale which describes you on the next page.

Ten represents your greatest agreement with the statement and one represents your least agreement. You should record your reaction quickly and without prolonged examination.

TEST E

1.	People consider me to be a competitive and successful person.
2.	I try to be efficient in my business and personal life.
3.	I believe failure and disgrace are some of the worse things that could happen to me.
4.	People often say that I am poised and self-reliant.
5.	People describe me as diplomatic, adaptable and ambitious.
6.	I sometimes expect others to assistance me in my ambitions.
7.	I endeavor to develop my abilities and talents more than most people do.
8.	I can get competitive with people.
9.	I am ambitious and often enjoy being the center of attention.
10.	I am more goal oriented than most people.

SCORE SHEET E

1.	1	2	3	4	5	6	7	8	9	10
	least agreement							most agreement		
2.	1	2	3	4	5	6	7	8	9	10
	least agreement							most agreement		
3.	1	2	3	4	5	6	7	8	9	10
	least agreement							most agreement		
4	1	2	3	4	5	6	7	8	9	10
	least agreement							most agreement		
5.	1	2	3	4	5	6	7	8	9	10
	least agreement							most agreement		
6.	1	2	3	4	5	6	7	8	9	10
	least agreement							most agreement		
7.	1	2	3	4	5	6	7	8	9	10
	least agreement							most agreement		
8.	1	2	3	4	5	6	7	8	9	10
	least agreement							most agreement		
9.	1	2	3	4	5	6	7	8	9	10
	least agreement							most agreement		
10.	1	2	3	4	5	6	7	8	9	10
	least agreement							most agreement		

Total your score for the circled numbers for these last ten questions here: _____

Read the statements below and determine your level of agreement with each statement. Circle the number on the scale which describes you on the next page.

Ten represents your greatest agreement with the statement and one represents your least agreement. You should record your reaction quickly and without prolonged examination.

TEST F

1. I would not like to live an average or commonplace type of life.

2. I see myself as a unique and creative person.

3. People see me as an emotional, feeling person.

4. I like to know what my feelings and urges are telling me.

5. I do not like conflicts with others and sometimes withdraw instead of fight.

6. I am sometimes inhibited and don't express myself to others.

7. I sometimes feel like I am an outsider.

8. I often observe and try to understand my feelings.

9. People usually do not understand my poetic sensibilities and deep feelings.

10. I am unique, romantic and have strong emotions.

SCORE SHEET F

1.	1	2	3	4	5	6	7	8	9	10
	least agreement							most agreement		
2.	1	2	3	4	5	6	7	8	9	10
	least agreement							most agreement		
3.	1	2	3	4	5	6	7	8	9	10
	least agreement							most agreement		
4	1	2	3	4	5	6	7	8	9	10
	least agreement							most agreement		
5.	1	2	3	4	5	6	7	8	9	10
	least agreement							most agreement		
6.	1	2	3	4	5	6	7	8	9	10
	least agreement							most agreement		
7.	1	2	3	4	5	6	7	8	9	10
	least agreement							most agreement		
8.	1	2	3	4	5	6	7	8	9	10
	least agreement							most agreement		
9.	1	2	3	4	5	6	7	8	9	10
	least agreement							most agreement		
10.	1	2	3	4	5	6	7	8	9	10
	least agreement							most agreement		

Total your score for the circled numbers for these last ten questions here: _____

Read the statements below and determine your level of agreement with each statement. Circle the number on the scale which describes you on the next page.

Ten represents your greatest agreement with the statement and one represents your least agreement. You should record your reaction quickly and without prolonged examination.

TEST G

1.	I prefer to gather all available information and then decide issues logically.
2.	I am a knowledgeable person and want to understand the world around me.
3.	I could not live a barren or meaningless life.
4.	I have restrained interpersonal skills and often don't share all my knowledge with others.
5.	I have few real close friends.
6.	I like to understand the way things work and strive to be an expert in my field of choice.
7.	I can be rather Spartan in my life and surroundings.
8.	I work best with little structure and am upset if given too much to do.
9.	I tend to avoid most physical sports.
10.	I usually do not express my emotions.

SCORE SHEET G

1.	1	2	3	4	5	6	7	8	9	10
	least agreement							most agreement		
2.	1	2	3	4	5	6	7	8	9	10
	least agreement							most agreement		
3.	1	2	3	4	5	6	7	8	9	10
	least agreement							most agreement		
4	1	2	3	4	5	6	7	8	9	10
	least agreement							most agreement		
5.	1	2	3	4	5	6	7	8	9	10
	least agreement							most agreement		
6.	1	2	3	4	5	6	7	8	9	10
	least agreement							most agreement		
7.	1	2	3	4	5	6	7	8	9	10
	least agreement							most agreement		
8.	1	2	3	4	5	6	7	8	9	10
	least agreement							most agreement		
9.	1	2	3	4	5	6	7	8	9	10
	least agreement							most agreement		
10.	1	2	3	4	5	6	7	8	9	10
	least agreement							most agreement		

Total your score for the circled numbers for these last ten questions here: _____

Read the statements below and determine your level of agreement with each statement. Circle the number on the scale which describes you on the next page.

Ten represents your greatest agreement with the statement and one represents your least agreement. You should record your reaction quickly and without prolonged examination.

TEST H

1.	I consider myself loyal.
2.	I am alert to the dangers around me.
3.	I follow the rules and like stability in my life.
4.	I like words, quotes and interesting phrases.
5.	I often have doubts and can feel insecure.
6.	I can be judgmental and critical when things go wrong.
7.	I sense the contradictions and ambiguities in life.
8.	I require logical proof of things and take little on faith.
9.	I am usually reliable, responsible and hardworking.
10.	Truth and justice are very important to me.

SCORE SHEET H

1.	1	2	3	4	5	6	7	8	9	10
	least agreement							most agreement		
2.	1	2	3	4	5	6	7	8	9	10
	least agreement							most agreement		
3.	1	2	3	4	5	6	7	8	9	10
	least agreement							most agreement		
4	1	2	3	4	5	6	7	8	9	10
	least agreement							most agreement		
5.	1	2	3	4	5	6	7	8	9	10
	least agreement							most agreement		
6.	1	2	3	4	5	6	7	8	9	10
	least agreement							most agreement		
7.	1	2	3	4	5	6	7	8	9	10
	least agreement							most agreement		
8.	1	2	3	4	5	6	7	8	9	10
	least agreement							most agreement		
9.	1	2	3	4	5	6	7	8	9	10
	least agreement							most agreement		
10.	1	2	3	4	5	6	7	8	9	10
	least agreement							most agreement		

Total your score for the circled numbers for these last ten questions here: _____

Read the statements below and determine your level of agreement with each statement. Circle the number on the scale which describes you on the next page.

Ten represents your greatest agreement with the statement and one represents your least agreement. You should record your reaction quickly and without prolonged examination.

TEST I

1.	Pain and suffering are among the worse things that could happen to me.
2.	I am optimistic and tend to deny the existence of my personal problems.
3.	I am talented in a variety of areas.
4.	I like myself and I'm usually good to myself.
5.	I am often busy planning for the next thing to do. My brain can jump from thing to thing.
6.	I don't like being told what to do and can sometimes have a difficult time with authority.
7.	I prefer to keep my options open and avoid circumstances that tie me down.
8.	I have knowledge of many different things and can talk at length about them.
9.	I am a good planner but often have difficulty in completing my projects.
10.	I generally enjoy life and am usually good-natured and lighthearted with others.

SCORE SHEET I

1.	1	2	3	4	5	6	7	8	9	10
	least agreement							most agreement		
2.	1	2	3	4	5	6	7	8	9	10
	least agreement							most agreement		
3.	1	2	3	4	5	6	7	8	9	10
	least agreement							most agreement		
4	1	2	3	4	5	6	7	8	9	10
	least agreement							most agreement		
5.	1	2	3	4	5	6	7	8	9	10
	least agreement							most agreement		
6.	1	2	3	4	5	6	7	8	9	10
	least agreement							most agreement		
7.	1	2	3	4	5	6	7	8	9	10
	least agreement							most agreement		
8.	1	2	3	4	5	6	7	8	9	10
	least agreement							most agreement		
9.	1	2	3	4	5	6	7	8	9	10
	least agreement							most agreement		
10.	1	2	3	4	5	6	7	8	9	10
	least agreement							most agreement		

Total your score for the circled numbers for these last ten questions here: _____

TEST Results

Transfer the scores from the nine personality answer sheets below:

Transfer the result from **test A** here: _____
This personality is called a **Perfectionist**.

Transfer the result from **test B** here: _____
This personality is called a **Champion.**

Transfer the result from **test C** here: _____
This personality is called a **Peacemaker.**

Transfer the result from **test D** here: _____
This personality is called a **Helper.**

Transfer the result from **test E** here: _____
This personality is called an **Achiever.**

Transfer the result from **test F** here: _____
This personality is called an **Artist.**

Transfer the result from **test G** here: _____
This personality is called an **Observer.**

Transfer the result from **test H** here: _____
This personality is called a **Loyalist.**

Transfer the result from **test I** here: _____
This personality is called an **Optimist.**

The test that has the highest score is your dominant personality type. The second highest score is your secondary personality type.

The anger brain personalities are:

A — the Perfectionist

B — the Champion

C — the Peacemaker

The emotional brain personalities are:

D — the Helper

E — the Achiever

F — the Artist

The fear brain personalities are:

G — the Observer

H — the Loyalist

I — the Optimist

Nine Personalities

This section is a preliminary view of your personality. It divides each of the three brain centers into three sub-centers that give us our basic nine personality types.

The ancient teaching of the three forces system is the foundation of the next subdivision of the personalities. They appear as active, passive or neutralizing and suspended.

Each of the three sub-centers directs their energy either as actively outward, passively inward or suspends it somewhere in between. Following this preliminary chapter, there will be an extensive chapter on each of the nine individual basic personalities.

The Quick View of Your Personality

The ancients discovered that each of the three brain centers have three different personality profiles. They noticed that each center could internalize, externalize or suspend their power. And each had its own unique personality.

The chart below shows how each of the nine personality types are related to each of the three dominate brains.

Three Brains	Suspend	External	Internal
Instinctive Anger, Group	Peacemaker	Champion	Perfectionist
Emotional Feeling Group	Achiever	Helper	Artist
Fear Logical Group	Loyalist	Optimist	Observer

With the test and your self observations, it is easier to begin the determination of your personality type by reading the short statements below. Even without the previous test, some people can narrow the choices to one or two possibilities just from this quick view. However, it is still recommended that you read the more detailed descriptions in chapter three to verify the determination of your personality type.

Instinctive Brain (Gut or Anger Group)

Peacemaker — Neutralize anger or suspend and replace anger with passive aggression.

Champion — Externalized anger projected outward towards others.

Perfectionist — Internalized anger projected inward towards self.

Emotional Brain (Heart or Feeling Group)

Achiever — Suspend and replace feelings with achievement.

Helper — Externalized feelings taking care of others.

Artist — Internalized feelings and dramatization of feelings.

Logical Brain (Head or Fear Group)

Loyalist — Fear suspended and projected onto the environment.

Optimist — Externalized fear diffused by many pleasant alternatives.

Observer — Internalized fear and afraid to experience it.

Expanded Description of Personality

Anger Center (instinctive brain)

Peacemakers are out of touch with their anger. They have a passive-aggressive type of anger. They are easy to be with, accommodating and see all sides of an issue. If they are umpires in a ball game they could decisively call ball or strike. Peacemakers usually do the right thing instinctively without thinking about it. They are fairly generous and easy going. Peacemakers are warm and have big hearts. They "are there" for others and don't appear to expect anything in return.

Champions are powerful and direct their anger outwardly. It is expressed as a hot anger. They readily let people know where they stand with them. What you see is what you get. They do not have a problem confronting things in their life. They focus on issues of their strength and other's weakness. In general, they do not play mind games. They can be really good friends and defenders of the weak. Beneath the hard outer shell of the Champion is usually a gentle, vulnerable heart.

Perfectionists direct their anger inwardly towards themselves. They believe anger is a character flaw and thus have a cold type of anger. They typically try to do what they think is the right thing. They are upright, fastidious and honest. They act on their own values as long as they believe they are in the right. They are careful and excel at meticulous tasks that don't necessarily require speed. They can have a good sense of humor about themselves, such as in the style of Johnny Carson. They generally hold their own ground around issues of moral principle. They probably had difficulty with the personality test because they wanted to circle exactly the right number.

Emotional or Relationship Center (emotional brain)

Achievers are out of touch with their emotions and instead strive to be seen in a good light. They are enthusiastic, competitive, hard working and give themselves fully to a job or task, with one hundred percent of their effort. They are goal or results oriented. They mingle and mix well in any group they choose. Achievers know how to present a desirable image and maintain a keen awareness of that image to the world around them.

Helpers direct their emotions outwardly. They are extroverts and sensitive to what others want, and they are caretakers of others. They are very empathic and sensitive to emotions and feelings. Relationships are their main concern or preoccupation. They often have a charming sense of silliness and playfulness in the style of Goldie Hawn. Helpers know how to impress others, and they are friendly, generous and can easily get people to like them. Many therapists are from the helper group.

Artists direct their emotions inwardly and have a need to be seen as special or original. They have a highly developed aesthetic sense. They are intensely in touch with deep feelings and the sadness and pain of existence and can be melancholic. They tend to be good artists of all kinds, actors, painters, singers and writers. They are well skilled in dramatic effects and use them often. Artists know how to make an entrance or exit. They will express themselves as unique individuals and usually have a good sense of style and fashion.

Fear Center (logical brain)

Loyalists are out of touch with their fear, and it is projected onto the environment. They tend to focus on those things that could go wrong. They control their fear by being vigilant of the possible dangers. They are dutiful and loyal and know who has the power in a group. They have a long attention span and are very logical about the things they do. They are good at planning and implementing strategies. Because they are out of touch with their fear, they are adventurous and take risks. They sometimes question authority and take an opposing point of view. They can be rebellious in a positive way.

Optimists direct their fear and energy outwardly and are extroverts. They diffuse the fear into pleasant options and can be charming and easy to get along with. They don't appear to have many problems and are generally pleasant and sociable. Optimists have dreams and visions of what's possible. They often have discriminating gourmet tastes in food, clothing and other things in life. They have a positive, upbeat approach to life and avoid disagreeable emotions and fear. They are good idea people, imaginative, prone to brainstorming, and they can be intellectuals.

Observers direct their fear and energy inwardly. They have a good sense of objectivity. They are aware of the value of things and the limitations of time and money. Observers minimize their needs and are efficient in their use of those resources at their disposal. They are independent and don't look to others to take care of them. Observers can be good listeners. They will not usually rock the boat or stir up trouble. They are often emotionally detached and tend to observe life without really participating in it.

To see all this more clearly, let's consider each personality in considerably more depth.

Chapter Three:
The Personality Types

This chapter provides a very expanded description of each of the nine personality types.

Perfectionist (Anger, Instinctive Brain)

Other Names That Could Be Used for the Perfectionist

- Improver
- Crusader
- Inspector
- Judge
- Resenter
- Reformer
- Corrector

Key to the Perfectionist Personality

- Most people avoid incompletion in their lives but Perfectionists excessively dislike and resist incompletion and imperfection in their lives.
- Instead, they replace incompletion and imperfection with a desire for things to be as they "should be".

Self Definition/Self Image
"I am right. I am hardworking."

Personality Traits

- Perfectionists do what they think is the right thing.
- Perfectionists don't like people who break the rules.
- They are inclined to see things as right or wrong, black or white.
- Perfectionists often try to reform or improve things.
- Perfectionists keep a tight rein on their emotions.
- Perfectionists often block real feelings with "shoulds and oughts".
- They are careful and excel at meticulous tasks.
- They are usually well organized.
- Perfectionists have strong self-discipline.
- Perfectionists strive to improve their situation.
- They are idealistic and feel strongly about their principles and beliefs.
- Perfectionists are people who usually try to do their best.
- They can be critical of themselves and others and have a fierce internal critic.
- Perfectionists have high standards for themselves and others.
- Perfectionists can have feelings of being unimportant or worthless.
- They like to improve things and work hard.

- They dread being judged or criticized by others.
- Perfectionists can express a cold simmering anger but they seldom allow it to boil over.

Preoccupations
- Demanding internal standards
- Comparing themselves to others
- Being concerned with criticism

Personality Strengths
Perfectionists do the right thing. Social pressures do not easily influence them if these go against what they think is right. They are not overly concerned if others like or dislike their actions. They act on their own values as long as they believe they are right. Mature Perfectionists have a sense of emotional calm, a tranquility or ease with themselves. They are careful and good at meticulous tasks. They can have a good sense of humor about themselves in the style of Johnny Carson. They generally hold their own ground around issues of principle.

Common Occupations
Perfectionists excel in those positions requiring skill, precision and correct action. They are often employed in the following roles: nurse, preacher, educator-teacher, accountant, engineer, technician, secretary, auto-mechanic, law enforcement, or quality control person.

Method of Communication
Perfectionists communicate by preaching, proselytizing, teaching, educating and moralizing. They can complain about what is wrong, more to change something rather than just resignation to the way things are. There conversations can project an attitude of telling others what to do for their own good.

Examples of International Perfectionists
England and Switzerland are Perfectionist countries. They are hard working and quite proper, generally showing little display of hot anger.

Examples of Perfectionist animals
The terrier, ant, and bee are examples of Perfectionists.

Typical Family History
Perfectionist children feel ignored on a deep emotional level. They get their special sense of self from their father and usually do not connect with the mother. The psychological message these children received was often "Be good. Behave yourself. Work hard. Don't be childish."

Possible Problems
People whose work or appearance is sloppy annoy perfectionists. They are easily upset by those who ridicule or criticize them.

Perfectionists have a tendency to believe they are the only people who can do anything right. Consequently, they resent other people whose performance does not meet their high standards. They can be judgmental and unwilling to be wrong and are often involved in conflicts. Perfectionists are emotionally unable to express their feelings and withhold these feelings instead of dealing with them.

When life is going especially bad, Perfectionists feel misunderstood and have a tendency to be depressed and to withdraw from others. They can feel lost and suffer from self-hate.

Peacemakers (Anger Center, instinctive brain)

Other Names That Could Be Used for the Peacemaker
- Mediator
- Negotiator
- Easygoer
- Acceptor
- Preservationist

Key to the Peacemaker Personality
- Most people avoid conflict in their lives but Peacemakers overly resist conflict and strife.
- Instead, they go with the flow and seek harmony and peace at almost any price.

Self Definition/Self Image
"I am easy going."

Personality Traits
- They are good at seeing both sides of an issue.
- Peacemakers tend not to sweat the small stuff.
- Peacemakers have big hearts.
- They can be there for others and don't expect anything in return.
- Peacemakers tend to put things off until almost the last minute.
- Peacemakers are "laid back", easy-going people.
- They are usually patient and unflappable.
- They prefer to work at their own pace.

- Peacemakers are balanced and "go with the flow".
- They are usually good listeners and diplomatic.
- Peacemakers are accepting and passive.
- They can numb themselves.
- Peacemakers are good at avoiding pressure.
- Peacemakers enjoy hanging out with their friends.
- They like to stay comfortable and undisturbed.

Preoccupations
- Experiencing conflict between positive belief and doubts often producing indecisiveness
- Difficulty saying "no"
- Adhering to others' desires as their means of finding security

Personality Strengths
Peacemakers are good at seeing both sides of an issue. They can make quick decisions. If they are umpires in a ball game they could decisively call ball or strike. Peacemakers usually do the right thing without thinking about it. They are fairly generous and easy going. Peacemakers have big hearts. They are there for others and don't expect anything in return.

Common Occupations
Peacemakers excel where they can perform routine work or within a lot of structure or where they can bring peace between conflicting people. They are often employed in the following occupations: detail work in a manufacturing

plant, arbitrator, diplomat, ambassador, administrator, public relations, bureaucrat.

Method of Communication
Peacemakers can tell long epic stories with far too many details. They also like to listen and to hear what is happening with others. They have a receptive, agreeable and complacent style. They can complain, not like a Perfectionist or a Champion, but a resigned complaining. They are usually not upset, but they can sometimes sound a little depressed. They can have a monotone voice. Their last sound in a sentence can drop down in pitch.

Examples of International Peacemakers
Barbados is an example of a Peacemaker personality country. Its people are patient, easy going and laid back.

Examples of Peacemaker Animals
Donkeys, elephants and sloths are examples of Peacemakers.

Typical Family History
Peacemakers can get their special sense of self from their mother and/or their father. Generally, they are not overly criticized or controlled as children but can be victims of benign neglect. Peacemaker children tend to perceive themselves as overlooked and not loved enough or listened to by their parents. Typically, the Peacemaker child's expression of anger did not produce its desired results; they consequently formed the habit of discounting their own essential needs. They interpreted their parents' messages as "Don't bother me. Don't exist. Go away."

Possible Problems
People who cause conflict or confront them upset peacemakers. Peacemakers tend to seek harmony at any cost. They can even ignore parts of reality in order to deny

any knowledge of conflict. This can often result in laziness, possibly sitting in front of the television and getting fat.

When life is going especially bad, Peacemakers experience self-doubt and have difficulty making decisions. They can be resistant to change and withdraw from life. They may have a tendency to despair and think life is too demanding and dangerous.

Champions (Anger Center, instinctive brain)

Other Names That Could Be Used for the Champion
- Boss
- Leader
- Statesman
- Chief
- Controller
- Dominator
- Challenger
- Self–reliant type
- Confronter
- Thrill seeker
- Asserter
- Questioner

Key to the Champion Personality
- Most people avoid weakness in their lives, but Champions overly resist weakness within themselves.
- Instead, they become powerful and stand up against others.

Self Definition/Self Image
"I can do it. I am powerful."

Personality Traits
- Champions let people know where they stand with them.
- They can be defenders of the underdog and the weak.
- Champions are assertive and want the world to notice them.
- They can be really good friends.

- Champions view life in terms of winning and losing.
- Champions work hard and know how to get things done.
- They are resourceful and want to be self-reliant.
- Champions generally are powerful, strong, self-confident people and will fight for what is right.
- They are proud, tough and domineering.
- They are direct and straightforward.
- Champions would rather be respected than liked.
- Decision making is easy for Champions.
- Champions tend to support the disadvantaged.
- They demand fairness and equality.
- They live life intensely.

Preoccupations
- Control of personal objects, space and people
- Excessive behavior: too loud, too late, too much
- Denying others' points of view in favor of a single legitimate opinion that supports the Champion's security

Personality Strengths
Champions let people really know where they stand with them. What you see is what you get. They have no problem in confronting life. In general, they do not play mind games. They can be really good friends. They can be defenders of the weak. Beneath the hard outer shell of the Champion is a soft, gentle wide-open heart.

Common Occupations

Champions excel in positions where they have a lot of power. They are often employed in the following occupations: armed forces sergeant or officer, police officer, attorney, sports athlete, union organizer, business manager.

Method of Communication

Champions are usually powerful, intimidating, unemotional and very direct in what they say and in the way they say it. They can use imperatives and might use a brash, earthy language, but not necessarily. They can sound arrogant and can complain about people who don't come up to their standards.

Examples of International Champions

Spain is an example of a Champion personality country. It is macho and rejects weakness.

Examples of Champion Animals

A rhinoceros, tiger, and bull are examples of Champions.

Typical Family History

Champions usually get their special sense of self from their mother. They tend to interpret the events of their childhood as feeling dominated by either a physically or an emotionally bigger or stronger person who wanted to control them. Champion children challenged this domination even though they had to fight against adults or older children representing overwhelming odds. They interpreted their early messages as "Don't be you. Don't feel what you feel."

Possible Problems

Weak people who won't stand up for themselves upset Champions. Champions will tend to be champions of justice, law, and order; Champions can fight to uphold these concepts. They deny they have any weaknesses and can scare others with their tough exterior.

When life is going especially bad, Champions have a tendency to withdraw and become introverted. They become stingy with their money, time and help for others. They might cheat or lie to others. If they become mentally unhealthy, Champions can become paranoid and dangerous, possibly getting into physical fights.

Helper (Relationship Center, Emotional Brain)

Other Names That Could Be Used for the Helper
- Giver
- Assistant
- Lover
- Nurturer
- Supporter
- Caretaker
- Pleaser

Key to the Helper Personality
- Most people avoid having excessive needs in their lives but Helpers overly resist feeling that they have personal needs.
- Instead, they take care of the needs of others and desire being needed and accepted by others.

Self Definition/Self Image
"I am helpful."

Personality Traits
- Helpers are very empathic and sensitive to the feelings and needs of others.
- Helpers know how to get people to like them.
- Helpers want to love and be loved.
- They are warm hearted and can be genuinely caring of others.
- They are usually dependable and keep their word

- Helpers want others to feel welcome and comfortable in their home or work environment.
- They are people pleasers and frequently compliment others.
- Helpers act more on feelings than logic but can also repress their feelings in order to be loved.
- They have difficulty recognizing their own needs.
- Helpers experience relationships as doing for others.
- Helpers can be self–sacrificing, giving up their own wants and needs for others.
- They are the most people–oriented of all the personality types.
- Helpers take pride in being needed and important in other people's lives.
- Helpers are normally caring and oriented toward helping or saving others.
- Helpers are very concerned with what others think of them.
- Helpers are generous with their feelings and time, and people often seek their comfort.

Preoccupations
- Gaining approval and avoiding rejection
- Pride in the importance of their giving to others
- Submitting to a powerful other person, then identifying with that person
- Altering oneself to meet the needs of other people

Personality Strengths

Helpers are very sensitive to various emotional levels. Helpers are very empathic and sensitive to the feelings of others. They are genuinely caring of others. Helpers are sensitive to what others want, and they are good at taking care of others.

Helpers often have a charming sense of silliness and playfulness in the style of Goldie Hawn. Helpers know how to impress others, and they generally know how to get people to like them, but they do not always desire to do it.

Common Occupations

Helpers excel in positions requiring sympathy and warmth. They are often employed in the following roles: social work, psychologist, physician, nurse, executive-secretary, teacher, minister.

Method of Communication

Helpers communicate by being emotional, giving compliments, help and advice. They like to talk about other people, their problems and their issues. They usually pay close attention to others while they talk. They also maintain good eye contact. They can quickly become intimate with details of your problems. They are the most likely to touch and hug others.

Examples of International Helpers

Tibet and the Philippines are Helper personality countries. Their people are typically helpful and kind.

Examples of Helper Animals

A licking puppy is an example of a Helper.

Typical Family History

Helpers get their special sense of self from their father, especially those female Helpers who may have been Daddy's special little girl. These children learn to keep the flow of love and attention coming their way with good and often manipulative behavior. Helpers perceive that people will like them if they are loving, pleasant and nice.

Possible Problems
People who do not need their help upset helpers. Helpers resent people who cause them to feel that they are intruding on their privacy. They dislike being ignored or disregarded and hate being unneeded. This stems from a feeling of being unworthy of love.

Helpers tend to believe they do not have needs, so they often project their real needs onto other people and try to help them. In the process, Helpers may feel they are the victims of life. Helpers want people to think of them as helpful and loving, but all the while they are attempting to manipulate other people.

If they become mentally unhealthy, Helpers have a tendency to want vengeance and control. They may either exhibit aggressive behavior or be unable to actually confront their enemies, instead developing physical or mental illnesses in order to get needed attention from others.

Achievers (Relationship Center, Emotional Brain)

Other Names That Could Be Used for the Achiever

- Succeeder
- Performer
- Motivator
- Administrator
- Marketer

Key to the Achiever Personality

- Most people avoid failure in their lives but Achievers overly resist failure and disgrace.
- Instead, they feel secure by identifying with success.

Self Definition/Self Image

"I am successful. I can accomplish many things."

Personality Traits

- Achievers mingle and mix well in any group they choose.
- They like to better and improve their image.
- They seek performance based approval rather than acceptance for who they are.
- Achievers know how to look good and are image-driven.
- They like recognition and awards.
- They are good at organizing their lives.
- Achievers work hard and give one-hundred percent to their efforts.

- Achievers are competitive and driven towards success.
- They set high goals, sustain a high level of productivity and are almost always busy doing something.
- Achievers present themselves well and make a good first impression.
- They are very goal oriented; they want to finish first.
- They are usually self-assured and cheerful and are rarely depressed.
- Achievers are concerned with how they appear to others.
- They are practical and efficient people.
- Achievers are self-assertive.
- They like to be busy and are sometimes called "doing people" or "Type A" personalities.
- Achievers can adapt to the expectations and values of others.

Preoccupations

- Identifying with competitive achievement
- Constantly adjusting their image in order to present the image that they think is desired
- Replacing genuine feelings with the current role they perform
- Deceiving themselves in order to maintain their sense of image
- Working on multiple tracks simultaneously

Personality Strengths
Achievers work hard, give themselves over to a job or task, and give it one hundred percent of their effort. They are goal oriented. Achievers mingle and mix well in any group they choose. Achievers know how to look good. They have an awareness of how they present themselves to the world.

Common Occupations
Achievers excel in positions requiring management or marketing/sales skills. They are often employed in the following occupations: marketing, sales, promotion, advertising, banking, entrepreneur, politician, acting, fashion, physician.

Method of Communication
Achievers talk professional, polished and are trendy. They tend to "self-promote" and talk about the great things that are going on in their lives. They will try to enroll you in doing what they are doing. Achievers sell themselves. They can have a positive lift at the end of a sentence.

They can speak very fast when they want to deliver a point. They sometimes say "Ah" to help them hold their turn to speak.

Examples of International Achievers
The United States is an Achiever personality country. It is very success oriented and rejects failure.

Examples of Achiever Animals
A Chameleon and a Peacock are examples of Achievers.

Typical Family History
Achievers get their special sense of self from their father, but to a less personal degree than Helper children.

They were prized for what they could produce or achieve rather than for being themselves.

Achiever children wanted their father's special attention but never quite seemed to get it. They therefore go into a performance role that never ends in an attempt to get the special attention. Achiever children don't get their special sense of self because of the individual person they are but rather for what things they can accomplish or achieve.

Possible Problems

Achievers can feel worthless and valueless by themselves, so they try to achieve external success. They can become upset with people who find faults with their work or who say they don't work hard enough.

Achievers tend to be efficient in getting many tasks completed but they have difficulty dealing with negative results. They compulsively avoid even the possibility of failure or anything else that makes them look bad in front of others.

When life is going especially bad, Achievers have a tendency to be out of touch with their emotions and to either become hostile or lazy, "space-out," and operate mechanically.

Artist (Relationship Center, Emotional Brain)

Other Names That Could Be Used for the Artist
- Romantic
- Unique
- Creator
- Creative type
- Individualist
- Visionary
- Special person
- Symbol maker

Key to the Artist Personality
- Most people dislike being average but Artists overly resist average or commonplace lives.
- Instead, they embellish their life so that they become unique, special and authentic.

Self Definition/Self Image
"I am unique and special and do not conform to ordinary standards."

Personality Traits
- Artists are often introspective, aesthetic, and see themselves as different from others.
- They are concerned with analyzing the feelings and motivations of themselves and others.

- Artists can cry easily and can be extremely affected emotionally by sorrow and pain.
- They can be moody and their feelings are easily hurt.
- They can be creative and appreciate the beauty of nature.
- Artists often seem to have dramatic events happening around them.
- Artists have difficulty being understood by others.
- They can over react to criticism.
- They have a highly developed artistic sense.
- Artists view life as a series of beginnings and endings.
- Artists may be on a quest to find the meaning of life.
- They have a good sense of style and flair.
- Artists are impatient with a mundane and ordinary life.
- They know what dramatic effect is and how to use it.
- They express themselves as individuals.
- They long for some missing ingredient in their life, such as a new lover or other difficult to get desire.
- Artists feel misunderstood by others.

Preoccupations
- Being attracted to what is distant and unavailable
- Experiencing sad or melancholy moods

- Being impatient with ordinary feelings
- Wanting to dramatize feelings through

a sense of loss

Personality Strengths

Artists are deeply in touch with the sadness and pain of existence. Artists tend to be good creators of any kind – acting, painting, singing and writing. They really know how to make an entrance or exit. They know what dramatic effect is and how to use it. Artists have a good sense of style and fashion. They express themselves as individuals.

Common Occupations

Artists excel in positions in the arts or in something creative. They are often employed in the following occupations: acting, dancing, painting, design, interior design, critic, entertainer, therapist, and counselor.

Method of Communication

Artists can tell lamenting, sad stories about their problems and the drama in their lives. They complain in a resigned way and with unhappiness in their voice. Their presentation can be dramatic, symbolic, and metaphorical.

Examples of International Artists

France is an example of an Artist personality country. It strives to be unique and different and to not conform to other international standards. The French have an "artistic temperament".

Examples of Artist Animals

A mourning dove and a noble black racing horse are examples of artist animals.

Typical Family History

Artists get their special sense of self from their father. They also remember being rejected or emotionally abandoned by their mother, which turns them towards their father. Their closeness to the father often contains an antagonist or negative energy. Artist children often hear their parents' messages as "Don't count on my being here for you. Don't be close," which caused them to retreat inward to their emotions and fantasies.

Possible Problems

Artists over-react to criticism. They dislike people who do not take them seriously when they are into their suffering moods. Artists tend to exaggerate or dramatize their life experiences in order to make themselves seem more interesting. They dislike feeling ordinary and will try to set themselves apart from others. Consequently, they often feel isolated and lacking in authenticity. They have difficulty with intimate relationships. Artists can spend time in fantasy instead of action.

When life is going especially bad, Artists can become morbid and have a tendency to attempt to attach themselves to other people. They are then more concerned with what other people think of them and their fear of rejection is increased. At their unhealthiest, they can become emotionally blocked and sometimes self-destructive through substance abuse addictions or even suicide.

Observers (Fear Center, Logical Brain)

Other Names That Could Be Used for the Observer
- Sage
- Thinker
- Knower
- Watcher
- Encyclopedia
- Hoarder

Key to the Observer Personality
- Most people avoid being incapable, but Observers overly resist being helpless and incapable.
- Instead, they fill themselves with many facts and lots of knowledge, trying to understand and get the "big picture".

Self Definition/Self Image
" I am perceptive and capable."

Personality Traits
- Observers are minimalists and aware of the value of things.
- They are independent.
- Observers will not usually rock the boat.
- They are often uneasy at parties and social gatherings and tend to be found in the back of the room.
- Observers view life as a problem to be solved.
- Observers are good at independent work.

- They live in their thoughts and have difficulty expressing feelings.
- Observers are usually private, low–profile people who avoid self-disclosure.
- They tend to concentrate and focus deeply on their own interests.
- They can stand back and view life dispassionately.
- They can easily spend time alone and are quite self-sufficient.
- They like privacy and a place where they can be alone and uninterrupted.
- They love acquiring knowledge.
- Observers usually keep their problems to themselves.
- They tend to be stingy with their knowledge and money.
- Observers are turned off by brash, loud people or events.

Preoccupations
- Being concerned with privacy
- Restricting or minimizing personal needs as a way of staying uninvolved
- Controlling unpredictable feelings and reactions
- Being interested in analytical knowledge as a substitute for emotional experience

Personality Strengths
Observers have a good sense of objectivity. They are aware of the value of things and the limitations of time and money. They are good conversationalists. Observers are efficient in their use of those resources at their disposal. They are independent and don't look to others to take care

of them. Observers can be good listeners. They will not usually rock the boat or stir up trouble. Observers are good at independent work or work that might require isolation.

Common Occupations

Observers excel in positions requiring logical thinking. They are often employed in the following occupations: librarian, research scientist, academic, archaeologist, computer worker, writer, accountant, staff worker, technician.

Method of Communication

Observers tend to say as little as possible. They can have a dry, detached and unemotional affect to their voice. They communicate about facts and information in a detached way. They report data without emotional involvement.

Examples of International Observers

Japan is an example of an Observer personality country. It is logical, frugal, and its people control their feelings and reactions.

Example of an Observer Animal

An owl is an example of observer animal.

Typical Family History

Observers often get more of their special sense of themselves from their mother, and get less contact from their father. One parent may have been either physically or emotionally intrusive. So Observer children closed down their feelings in order to get away from this oppression. They interpreted their parents' messages as "Don't be close. Don't belong."

Possible Problems

Observers become upset with people who are pushy and make demands on them. Observers tend to over accumulate knowledge. They can feel despair and withdraw from others, becoming observers of life instead of participants.

When life is going especially bad, Observers have a tendency to plan and daydream more, while rarely actually following through with the plans. If they become mentally unhealthy, they can be antagonistic towards those who are critical of their dreams or beliefs. They might identify with radical causes or ideas. Observers can become paranoid and frightened by life.

Loyalists (Fear Center, Logical Brain)

Other Names That Could Be Used for the Loyalist Personality

- Defender
- Problem Finder
- Supporter
- Questioner
- Guardian
- Loyal Skeptic
- Facilitator
- Doubter
- Devil's Advocate
- Groupist

Key to the Loyalist Personality

- Most people avoid rejection in their lives but Loyalists overly resist separation or rejection from family or a group.
- Instead, they find security by learning to be loyal and to avoid the disapproval of their chosen group. However, they sometimes question or challenge authority for constructive purposes.

Self Definition/Self Image

"I am loyal. I am cautious."

Personality Traits

- Loyalists need security and certainty.
- They have a long attention span.
- Loyalists can be rebellious, usually in a positive way.

- They are good at planning and implementing strategies.
- They are usually on the alert for danger.
- Loyalists are hard working and take their responsibilities seriously.
- Loyalists view life as threatening.
- Loyalists want to be safe and to overcome fears.
- Loyalists can be afraid of being abandoned.
- They like predictability.
- Loyalists look for common ground between themselves and others.
- Loyalists usually believe in loyalty and duty.
- Loyalists have a sense of tradition.
- They can have difficulty making decisions.
- Loyalists believe life can be very demanding, and they are very sensitive to dangers.
- They require logical proof of things.
- They may have a nervous energy about them.

Preoccupations
- Being alert to danger
- Facing issues with authority – whether to submit or rebel
- Procrastinating instead of doing
- Being suspicious of others' motives
- Scanning the environment for clues that explain their inner sense of impending danger

Personality Strengths

Loyalists have a long attention span and can really be careful and pay attention to the things they are doing. They are good at planning and implementing strategies. They are adventurous and take risks. Loyalists can be rebellious in a positive way. They can question authority, stand up to authority, and take an opposing point of view, as long as it is for the good of the group.

Common Occupations

Loyalists excel in positions that have logical methods for determining the correct course of action. They are often employed in the following occupations: instructor at school, engineer, armed forces officers, policeman, fireman, attorney, government jobs, machinist, builder, scientist.

Method of Communication

Loyalists often talk about the group they are in. They can be rebellious or provocative and argue with you on an analytical level, weighing the pros and cons. They can caution you to be suspicious and take heed of various dangers. Their speech pattern might be halting. Loyalists might take big breaths and speak a long time on each breath.

Examples of International Loyalists

Germany is an example of a Loyalist personality country. It is loyal and has safety and security issues.

Examples of Loyalist Animals

A wolf, or a loyal German shepherd are examples of Loyalists.

Typical Family History

Loyalists get their special sense of self from their mother. Loyalist children are often raised with ambiguous rules with limits not clearly defined. One wrong step might be disastrous and they never knew which step that will be. Parents tend to have inconsistent rules. The Loyalist children heard their parents' messages as "Don't do that. Be careful. If you don't watch out, it'll get you."

Possible Problems

Loyalists become upset with people who dispute their reality. They also react negatively to people who appear to be feeble-minded.

Loyalists tend to run from their fear and seek their security in their family or in groups. They dislike deviations from any group ethics that would threaten the group and hence their security.

When life is going especially poorly, Loyalists have a tendency to be more anxious about how they appear to others. They can feel more incompetent and seem unable to act on their own. They complain more about their problems. If they become mentally unhealthy, Loyalists could become self-destructive, or they might become aggressive towards others.

Optimists (Fear Center, Logical Brain)

Other Names That Could Be Used for the Optimist
- Visionary
- Adventurer
- Planner
- Generalist
- Fun Lover
- Epicurean
- Enjoyer
- Cheerer
- Enthusiast
- Dreamer
- Networker
- Materialist

Key to the Optimist Personality
- Most people avoid pain and suffering in their lives but Optimists overly resist pain, suffering and boredom.
- Instead, they avoid pain by focusing on pleasure, opportunity and planning for the future and focusing on happy things.

Self Definition/Self Image
"I am fun. I see the bright side of life."

Personality Traits
- Optimists can be charming and easy to get along with.
- They are optimists and have dreams and visions of what is possible.
- Optimists are free–spirited and spontaneous.

- They look for the awe and wonder in life.
- They often have discriminating taste in food, clothing and many other areas of life.
- Optimists dislike authority but usually avoid conflicts with authority by removing themselves from the problem.
- They love travel, new adventures and excitement.
- Optimists see life as having endless possibilities.
- They want to keep their options open and dislike limits.
- They have knowledge about many subjects and can "wear many hats".
- Optimists love to celebrate life.
- They have many interesting things to do in their calendar.
- Optimists pursue stimulation and peak experiences.
- They often have lots of new ideas.
- Optimists are usually lively and talkative.
- Optimists tend to work in spurts.

Preoccupations
- Maintaining a high level of stimulation and activities in order to stay feeling "high"
- Planning and intellectualizing
- Diffusing negative feelings by maintaining a smoke screen of activity
- Using charm as the first line of defense against fear

Personality Strengths

Optimists can be charming and easy to get along with. They don't have many problems and are generally pleasant and social. They can be intellectuals. Optimists have dreams and visions of what's possible. They often have discriminating taste in food, clothing and many other areas. They have a positive, upbeat approach to life. They are good idea people and imaginative brain stormers.

Common Occupations

Optimists excel in planning or researching new concepts. They are better in staff positions than line positions. They are often employed in the following occupations: consultant, management staff, sales, public relations, storyteller, comedian, entrepreneur, writer, scientist.

Method of Communication

Optimists are good conversationalists. They usually conduct enthusiastic, friendly, agreeable discussions about ideas. They are good storytellers, and can get you involved in their personal stories. Optimists tend not to talk about feelings. Instead, they talk about plans and theories on an intellectual and abstract level.

Examples of International Optimists

Ireland is an example of an Optimist personality country. It looks at the bright side of life and even celebrates after funerals. Brazil is another example of an Optimist country with its carnivals and attitude of celebration.

Examples of Optimist Animals

A monkey is an example of an Optimist.

Typical Family History

Optimists get their special sense of self from their mother. They were probably Mother's special person and during some early point in their life this special connection was lost leaving a deep fear. Still, Optimists remembers their childhood as pleasant and are usually out of touch with the fear and any pain that might have occurred while they were growing up. Optimists are left with the feeling that they can't quite trust life and want a backup "Plan B".

Possible Problems

Optimists don't like being deprived of anything. They are upset by people who try to force or manipulate them to do things that are not fun.

Optimists tend to make many plans but actually carry out few of these plans. They dream rather than do the work necessary for their plans to reach completion.

When life is going especially bad, Optimists have a tendency to be resentful of what life is dealing them. They cease their usual optimism and find fault with things. They might become rude and aggressive. They may try to forget their anxieties by addictions to food, sex, alcohol or drugs. When giving up one vice or bad habit, they tend to indulge in another.

Chapter Four: Further Into The Personalities

Personality Types of Famous People

None of the people mentioned here took the tests in this book, so assigning them to particular personality types involved a certain amount of educated and—we hope—inspired guesswork. The greatest potential for error is contained in the amount by which a celebrity's authentic private personality differs from their public image. These personality type assignments were made solely according to public image—indeed, a few are of fictional characters.

It is possible that if we knew more about the real characteristics of some of these prominent people, we would assign them to a different personality type. However, it's reasonable to believe that the public image associated with a person is not there by accident, and that it does provide some kind of window into that person's soul.

Examples of Famous Perfectionists

William F. Buckley, Tom Smothers, Johnny Carson, Dr. Jeckyll (Mr. Hyde is a Champion), Barbara Walters, Katherine Hepburn, Confucius, Audrey Hepburn, Tom Brokaw, H. Ross Perot, John Grisham, William F. Buckley, Ralph Nader, President Harry Truman, Margaret Thatcher, Al Gore, Marcia Clark, Joan Baez, Harrison Ford, Jerry Seinfeld, Jodie Foster, Ross Perot, Dr. Laura Schlesinger, Margaret Thatcher, Brian Williams, Mr. Spock from Star Trek, Condoleezza Rice

Examples of Famous Peacemakers

Hubert Humphrey, Julia Child, Clint Eastwood, Gerald Ford, George Burns, Walt Disney, Walter Cronkite, Dwight Eisenhower, Jean Stapleton, Dwight Eisenhower, Joseph Campbell, Peter Falk, Dean Martin, Abraham Lincoln, Sandra Bullock, Laura Bush, Kevin Costner, Jerry Seinfeld, Gloria Steinem, Bob Woodward, Charles Bronson, Johnny Cash, James Brown

Examples of Famous Champions

President Donald Trump, President Theodore Roosevelt, George Patton, Winston Churchill, John Wayne, Bill O'Reilly, Beethoven, Fritz Pearls, Mr. T, Henry Vlll, Joan Rivers, Pablo Picasso, Dictator Fidel Castro, Rush Limbaugh, Ernest Hemingway, Jimmy Hoffa, Danny DeVito, Rhea Perlman, George C. Scott, Golda Meir, Charles Bronson, Lee Marvin, Mike Wallace, F. Lee Bailey, Lee Iacocca, Napoleon Bonaparte, China Dictator Mao Tse-tung, Apache leader Geronimo, Denzel Washington, Pablo Picasso, George Gurdjieff, Indira Gandhi, President Lyndon Johnson

Examples of Famous Helpers

Monica Lewinsky, Jerry Lewis, Barbara Bush, Dolly Parton, Eva Peron, Goldie Hawn, Bill Cosby, Elton John, Eleanor Roosevelt, Monica Lewinsky, Mr. Rogers, Mother Teresa, Leo Buscaglia, Melanie Griffith, Alan Alda, Sally Jessy Raphael, Suze Orman, Sally Struthers, Ken Burns, Debbie Reynolds, Richard Simmons, Farrah Fawcett

Examples of Famous Achievers

Michael Jordan, Elvis Presley, Arnold Schwartzenegger, President Bill Clinton, Montel Williams, Tony Blair, Tony Robbins, Werner Erhard, Tiger Woods, Tom Cruise, Dick Clark, Cybill Shepherd, Bryant Gumbel, Jamie Lee Curtis, Johnny Cochran, Muhammad Ali, Jesse Jackson, Paul

McCartney, Mick Jagger, David Bowie, Lance Armstrong, Tom Cruise, Tiger Woods

Examples of Famous Artists
Bob Dylan, Janis Joplin, Neil Young, Brian Ferry, Leslie Howard, Daniel Day Lewis, Neil Diamond, Joni Mitchell, James Dean, Vanessa Redgrave, Michelangelo, Alan Watts, Orson Welles, Michael Jackson, Marilyn Manson, Hank Williams, Tennessee Williams, Gloria Steinem, Neil Diamond, Edgar Allen Poe, Alan Watts, Cher, Marlon Brando, Cat Stevens, Ingmar Bergman, Michael Jackson, Nicolas Cage, Vincent Van Gogh

Examples of Famous Observers
Albert Einstein, Chopin, Emily Dickinson, Howard Hughes, Henry Fonda, T. S. Eliot, Issac Asimov, John D. Rockefeller, Bill Gates, Nikola Tesla, Stephen King, George Lucas, Bobby Fischer, Buddha, John D. Rockefeller, Thomas Edison, Stanley Kubrick, George Lucas, Bobby Fisher, Stephen Hawking

Examples of Famous Loyalists
Sigmund Freud, Krishnamurti, Richard Nixon, Tom Clancy, Woody Allen, Sally Field, Ted Turner, David Letterman, Rush Limbaugh, Marilyn Monroe, Phil Donahue, Sonny Bono, Julia Roberts, Mark Twain, Mel Gibson, Tom Hanks John Grisham, Mel Gibson, Suzanne Somers, Steve McQueen, Bob Newhart, George Bush, Newt Gingrich, Neil Young, Robert Redford

Examples of Famous Optimists
Carl Sagan, Henry David Thoreau, Kurt Vonnegut, Jack Nicholson, Ram Dass, Whoopie Goldberg, Jeff Bezos, Timothy Leary, President John F. Kennedy, Loni Anderson, Steven Spielberg Steve Allen, Chevy Chase, Joseph Campbell, Tanya Tucker, Alan King, Tom Hanks, Dick Van Dyke, Cameron Diaz, Howard Stern, Jonathan Winters, Peter

O'Toole, Jay Leno, Duke Ellington, Alan King, Tom Hanks, Charlie Rose, Robin Williams, Orsen Wells

Childhood Influences

Nature or nurture? It has been argued for decades whether children are born with a genetic personality (nature) or learn a personality from their environment (nurture). Most authorities today agree that both processes take place. As very young children, both our genetic heritage and our environment help shape our personality. In some cases, one may clearly predominate over the other.

No one knows how much of that our personality type we inherit from our parents through genes. It is reasonable to assume that we pick much of it up in our early environment. But this does not mean that as children our parents do not influence our environment and personality type. They do, and very strongly, by contributing to what we feel when we think about ourselves as individuals.

Early in life, children develop a special sense of self. One factor that is a great influence on children's personality is where their sense of self comes from. Usually this is from a parent or substitute parent, such as a grandparent or older relative living with the family. Children can get their special sense of self from a parent, even if little time is spent with this parent, or even if this is not the favorite parent.

The following are the most clear-cut general personality relations between parents (or substitute parents) and offspring.

Children attempt to resolve their fundamental needs from their environment. In their attempts to make sense of this environment, they begin to function as one of the nine different personality types. The childhood scenarios that follow may seem somewhat negative, but it is a child's preoccupation with these perceived negatives that influences their development into particular personality types. The circumstances and details can be expected to vary widely with individuals.

Perfectionists

Perfectionists usually get their special sense of self from their father. They have often felt emotionally abandoned by both parents at an early age. The Perfectionist child need not have been close to the father to be deeply influenced by him. The mother may have been ill or preoccupied by divorce or emotional issues, or some other circumstances may have been responsible for the lack of emotional closeness between her and the child.

Sometimes the Perfectionist child has been required to assume grown-up responsibilities and care for younger members of the family. Such children perceive the expectation that they must be well behaved, follow rules, constantly improve, and not get angry. They tend to bond to rules and to have a difficult time knowing what real emotional connectedness is.

Both Perfectionist and Peacemaker children tend to have been ignored, but Perfectionist also may have been much more criticized, or in extreme cases even abused, for failing to live up to their parents' standards.

Champions

Usually Champions get their special sense of self from their mother. They have often come from families that attempted to over dominate their life, either physically or emotionally. They have challenged this domination, even though they had to fight adults or older children representing overwhelming odds. Champions may deny they had a bad childhood but admit they had to struggle against powerful people. Some Champions have been emotionally abandoned children.

Peacemakers

Either the father or mother gives the sense of self to Peacemakers. As children, typical Peacemakers perceive themselves as not loved enough or listened to by their parents, and possibly even see them-selves as emotionally abandoned. They have often been the firstborn who got lost as the other children come along. They may have had to take care of the other children, like a third parent, and lacked enough personal attention for themselves. Generally, they have not been as criticized or controlled as Perfectionist children, but are victims of benign neglect. Sometimes Peacemakers have been the youngest child and were treated mechanically and ignored. Peacemakers tend to believe they have taken a back seat to other members of the family. They have probably not been given a strong sense of themselves as children, and typically their shows of anger never produced desired results.

Helpers

Helpers have a very special tie with their father, especially females who have been Daddy's little girl. Helpers have needed their father's attention and tried to be what he wanted them to be. In cases where he was distant, the Helper child tried even harder. As children, Helpers have probably felt emotionally insecure about their mother. When feeling ill or sad, they have tried to look all right in order to please their father. They have perceived that people like them if they are loving, pleasantly spoken, and nicely behaved.

Achievers

Achievers are less strongly influenced by their father than Helpers. Although Achievers as children have tried to get their father's attention by what they could do, they never seem to have fully succeeded in getting it, with the result that they have slipped into an endless attention-seeking performance role. As children, Achievers do not get their special sense of self from consciousness of their individuality but from what they can accomplish or achieve.

Artists

Besides getting their special sense of self from their father, Artists often experience an emotional abandonment, or in extreme cases a physical abandonment, by their mother. This increases the closeness to the father and perhaps contributes to its frequently antagonistic, distorted, or negative quality that results in an unhappy childhood. As children, Artists retreat inward in emotions and fantasies.

Observers

Getting their special sense of self from their mother, Observers as children tend to perceive their father as scary and distant. They have often been relatively ignored by both parents. Perhaps they were even told to stay out of the way by their mother. In early childhood, they have had a powerful experience of unfulfilled need, for example, not enough milk at the breast, not enough time with parents, or not enough holding and affection. The children have wanted to be angry with this but have found anger to be too frightening an emotion.

Loyalists

The mother is the most influential parent for Loyalists. Unlike Perfectionist children, who have been brought up with clear rules, Loyalist children have been raised with ambiguous rules. Their parents have laid down inconsistent rules, with limits not clearly defined. The children have come to feel that rules are a minefield in which it is easy to break a rule you didn't even know existed—with dire consequences. One wrong step can be disastrous, and you never know which step that will be. As children, Loyalists are closer to the mother and may be afraid of the father.

Optimist

The mother gives the special sense of self to the Optimist. They have probably been Mother's special person, but at some early stage of their life, this special connection has been lost. This may have been caused by the birth of another child or the return of the mother to work. The perceived loss has left a yearning to restore the original close tie to the mother, and the child may have tried to reestablish such a connection with another woman, such as a grandmother or aunt. Such children, feeling their loss and tend to direct their anger toward their father rather than their mother.

Before the withdrawal of the mother's attention, the child may have been enrolled in "saving" the mother or making her life complete. The child keeps trying to be pleasant to the mother in order to get back that special tie, but underneath has a sense of emotional abandonment. The child does not want to rely on pleasantness alone and wants a backup plan. Optimists usually have pleasant childhood memories, in particular of their mother.

Gentle Persuasion

You hear people talk of pressing other people's emotional buttons, electronic age lingo for the ancient art of persuasion or seduction. Each of the nine personality types is susceptible to particular kinds of emotional manipulation. This need not always be interpreted in the injurious sense, since the emotional manipulation may be benevolent and undertaken by someone who cares deeply.

We all, even the strongest and most independent, have our areas of emotional vulnerability. And those who wish to affect us most deeply, out of either love or hate, can do so most easily by probing these regions. But this does not always have to be at a profound level. For example, a little flattery where it counts can be all that's needed to clinch some minor business transaction—or get you invited somewhere you are curious to see.

Here is a quick guide to the ways in which each personality type, including your own, can most easily be persuaded.

Perfectionists

You can flatter Perfectionists by asking them questions and treating their answers respectfully. They like to teach and have their opinion sought. You can break the ice with a Perfectionist by telling a tasteful joke.

Champions

Be open and honest with Champions. Speak up for yourself. They will be the ones asking you how they can help.

Peacemakers

Peacemakers are flattered if you pay them attention and include them as central people in your activities.

Peacemakers like to help you, but don't expect anything in return for their help.

Helpers

More than any other personality type, Helpers love affection. They seek your approval and want your validation. Pat them on the back and let them know they are liked or loved for who they are. Once they know they are needed, they will do things for you, as long as you show recognition and appreciation.

Achievers

Achievers enjoy being admired for how happy and successful they look. All you have to do is applaud them for their beauty and achievements.

Artists

Artists know how unique and special they are. They will especially enjoy your compliments on their esthetic taste. Your continued support, compliments, and friendship, particularly during times when they are saying offensive things about you, are deeply appreciated, as is your sympathy when they are suffering.

Observers

Observers want you, and everyone else, to be impressed with their vast knowledge and in awe of their wisdom. Take it from there.

Loyalists

Let Loyalists know you respect them because they are creative, intelligent, loyal, and sexy.

Optimists

Optimists want you to experience the good things in life with them. Unfortunately, this may include participating in their many dreams and plans for the future.

Occupations And Problems

No single personality is better than another. All nine personality types have their positive and negative aspects. Certainly, nothing in the tests you have taken is intended to pass judgment on anyone. What the tests can do for you is make you more aware of your strengths and weaknesses. Once you recognize them, you are in a better position to make allowances for yourself where you do not have great strength, and to take advantage of those areas in which you are more capable or confident than most people.

For each personality type, certain occupations are more congenial. Anyone can work in any occupation, but some jobs are more of a stretch and needlessly stressful for some personality types. In this chapter, we look at the kinds of work for which the nine personality types are most suited and unsuited.

Likewise, anyone can get along with anyone else, but some personality types interact more easily with others. You naturally relate well with certain personality types, and these people most easily become your Mends or partners. People who belong to personality types other than these require more effort on your part for closer and satisfying relation-ships. Knowing another person's personality type can go far in explaining either the good or bad feelings that exist between you and him or her. The other personality types with which you are most likely to get along are given in this chapter.

Problems are often a matter of how you perceive life. A minor annoyance or even a challenge can something causes perfectionist personalities major anxiety. Your personality is often responsible for how you look at things—whether you see a person or an event as pleasant, unpleasant, or neutral. The things most likely to arise as problems in your life are discussed in this chapter according to personality type.

A healthy life is dynamic, seldom static. When we are really living our lives to the fullest, we are always growing and changing, even when we do not realize it. The indications of active personal growth are given for each personality type.

Perfectionist

Occupations: Perfectionists have difficulty with work involving many different conflicting ideas, such as being a judge or producer.

Perfectionists excel in positions requiring skill and precise and correct ways of doing the job, for example, as a physician, nurse, clergyman, teacher, accountant, technician, librarian, or secretary.

Interactions Perfectionists get along easiest with other Perfectionists, helpers, Optimists, Champions and Peacemakers

Problems: Perfectionists are upset by people who are sloppy about their work or appearance. They are easily annoyed by those who ridicule or criticize them.

They tend to believe they are the only people who can do anything right. Consequently, they resent others whose performance does not meet their high standards. They can become judgmental, unwilling to be wrong, and involved in conflicts. Often perfectionists are unable to express their feelings, and they withhold these feelings instead of dealing with them.

When life presents difficulties—at home or at work—Perfectionists feel misunderstood and tend to be depressed and to withdraw from others. They can feel lost and suffer from self-hate.

Champions

Occupations: Champions have a lot of difficulty with jobs like those in factories, where they are the underdogs who must follow orders, and are not in a position of power.

Champions excel in positions where they have a lot of power, for example, as a commissioned or noncommissioned officer in the armed forces, police officer, attorney, sports figure, businessman, union organizer, and business manager.

Interactions: Champions achieve the most easygoing interactions with other Champions, Perfectionists, Helpers, Observers, Optimists, and Peacemakers.

Problems: Champions have no time for weak people who won't stand up for themselves. They are often champions of justice or law and order. Denying they have any weaknesses, they scare others with their tough exterior.

When they are disappointed, Champions often withdraw and become introverted. They become stingy with their money, time, and help for others, and may cheat or lie. Mentally unhealthy Champions can be paranoid and physically dangerous.

Peacemakers

Occupations: Peacemakers have difficulty in jobs that require a bold statement, such as a fashion model, or that require quick movement from one situation to another, such as a quarterback, or that require self-promotion, as in sales.

Peacemakers are most contented where they can perform routine work with a lot of structure or where they can act as a peacemaker between conflicting sides. They are suited to the position of arbitrator, ambassador, administrator, bureaucrat, and umpire or referee, and also do well in public relations and at detail work in a laboratory or manufacturing plant.

Interactions: Peacemakers get along most easily with other Peacemakers, Perfectionists, Achievers, Loyalists, and Champions.

Problems: Peacemakers are upset by people who regularly cause conflict. Seeking harmony at any cost, they can even ignore reality in an effort to deny the existence of conflict. This often results in laziness.

When events go badly for Peacemakers, they experience self-doubt and have even more difficulty making decisions. They can be resistant to change and withdraw from life, and they can become depressed and think that life is too demanding and dangerous.

Helpers

Occupations: Helpers are not suited to professions with a high risk of disapproval or, loss of popularity, such as politics or law enforcement.

Helpers do well in positions requiring sympathy and warmth, for example, as a social worker, psychologist, physician, nurse, executive secretary, or clergyman.

Interactions: Helpers get on best with other Helpers, Perfectionists, Achievers, Artists, Observers, and Champions.

Problems: Helpers can be upset by people who do not need and reject their help. They resent people who cause them to feel that they are intruding on their privacy. They dislike being ignored or disregarded, and hate being unneeded.

Helpers tend to believe that they themselves do not have needs, and so they often project their real needs onto other people and then try to help them. In the process, helpers may feel they are victims of life. They want people to think of them as helpful and loving, but all the while they are attempting to manipulate others, who may therefore resent them.

If they become mentally unhealthy, Helpers often want vengeance. They may become aggressive or, if unable to actually confront their "enemies," develop physical or further mental sickness in order to get needed attention from others.

Achievers

Occupations: Achievers do not feel comfortable with employment that requires a socially unpopular viewpoint, such as a criminal lawyer or worker for a protest group.

Achievers have excellent management skills, meaning they can convince others to do things. Among the jobs they enjoy are acting, medicine, marketing, sales, promotion, advertising, corporate management, banking, entrepreneurship, and politics.

Interactions: Achievers interact best with other Achievers, Helpers, Artists, Loyalists, and Peacemakers.

Problems: Achievers become upset with people who find fault with their work or who say they don't work hard enough.

Achievers get multiple tasks completed efficiently, but they have difficulty dealing with negative results. They compulsively avoid even the possibility of failure or anything else that makes them look bad in front of others.

When things don't work out, Achievers get out of touch with their feelings and can become either hostile or lazy, spaced out, and robot-like.

Artists

Occupations: Artists do not like jobs that make them feel like a small cog in the wheel or that in any way remind them they are not unique, such as in a low-level position.

Artists are creative and do well in the arts, for example, in acting, dancing, painting, and interior decoration. They also do well as critics, entertainers, and counselors.

Interactions: Artists relate most easily with other Artists, Perfectionists, Helpers, Achievers, and Observers.

Problems: Artists overreact to criticism and, when they are into their suffering moods, dislike people who do not take them seriously. They like to exaggerate or dramatize their life experiences in order to make themselves seem more interesting. They don't like feeling ordinary and try to set themselves apart from others. Consequently, they feel isolated and lacking in authenticity. Artists have difficulty with intimate relationships, and can spend time in fantasy instead of action.

When things do not go their way, Artists often become morbid and try to attach themselves to people. Because they are more concerned at such times with what other people think of them, their fear of rejection is increased. At their worst, they can become emotionally blocked and self-destructive through drugs or even suicide.

Observers

Occupations: The jobs that Observers find stressful are those with high visibility, such as a television reporter, and those in which their boss can determine exactly how well they do each day, as in sales.

Observers excel in positions that need logical thinking, such as accountant, computer programmer, writer, librarian, re-search scientist, archaeologist, or other academic position.

Interactions: Observers have their most easily satisfying relationships with other Observers, Helpers, Artists, Loyalists, and Champions.

Problems: Observers get upset with pushy people who make demands on them. They often accumulate knowledge in order to fill their empty lives. Feeling despair and withdrawing from others, they can become mere observers of life instead of true participants.

If life gets tough, Observers believe they should plan their way out of trouble but often daydream instead of following through on their plans. They may become antagonistic toward those who are critical of their dreams or beliefs. They may identify with radical causes or ideas, and can become paranoid and frightened.

Loyalists

Occupations: Positions that involve serious judgment calls, such as those of judge or doctor, create great tensions for Loyalists, as do jobs that involve under-the-table manipulations or highly competitive environments.

Loyalists do best where logical methods exist for determining the correct course of action. Examples are a school instructor, engineer, officer in the armed forces, police officer, firefighter, civil servant, machinist, builder, or technologist.

Interactions: Loyalists require less effort to get along with other Loyalists, Achievers, Observers, Optimists, and Peacemakers.

Problems: Loyalists react negatively to people who see things differently or who appear to be feebleminded.

Loyalists tend to run from their fears and seek security in the family or a group. They dislike deviations from group ethics that might threaten the group and therefore their security.

In times of adversity, Loyalists tend to be increasingly anxious about how they appear to others. They feel more incompetent, seem unable to act on their own, and complain more about their problems. Loyalists can become self-destructive or become aggressive toward others when mentally unhealthy.

Optimists

Occupations: Optimists have difficulty with routine employment (such as that of a factory weaker), where they have to take care of the details while they are controlled by a supervisor who does all the planning for them.

Optimists are most at home in positions that necessitate planning or researching new concepts. They are better in staff jobs than line jobs. Suggested jobs and fields include consultant, editor, management staff, sales, public relations, entrepreneur, writer, and scientist.

Interactions: Optimists naturally relate well to other Optimists, Perfectionists, Observers, Loyalists, and Champions.

Problems: Optimists get riled by people who try to force or manipulate them to do things that aren't fun.

Optimists like to make many plans but actually carry out few of them. They dream rather than do the work necessary for their plans to reach fruition.

When life deals Optimists a poor hand, they tend to be resentful, lose their usual optimism, and find fault with things. They may become rude and aggressive, or try to forget their anxieties through sex, drink, drugs, or food. When giving up one vice or bad habit, they often substitute another.

Possible Profiles

No approach to human personality enables us to attach labels to people with the expectation that they will henceforth behave according to rigid specifications. This personality system is not meant to be used as a branding iron, so that people can never erase the personality stamped on their hide. Rather than limit or confine, this system opens up psychic territory. It can be thought of as an investigative tool, something like Sherlock Holmes's magnifying glass or a radio telescope aimed into deep space to receive tantalizing and sometimes mysterious signals.

With the caution that no system has yet succeeded in classifying humans into watertight compartments, and keeping in mind that people rarely behave exactly as we expect or think they should. Nine short biographies are presented here, one for each of the nine personality types. The biographies may help the reader visualize what the personality types look like in flesh and blood.

Who are these people? Are they real or are they composite portraits, each one made up of the necessary ingredients of a particular personality type, like the recipe for a dish? They are all real. None are homogenized blueprints.

Being very real people, these individuals fit their personality type in different ways and to different degrees of completeness. But imperfect as they are, they are from real life—from what awaits you beyond the pages of this book.

Perfectionist

At twenty-two, Bonnie is unmarried and works as a ticket agent for a large airline. She is responsible and hardworking, trying to get every detail right in order to please people. Although she has high standards, she is not ambitious, being quite satisfied at her present job level. She wants to be financially comfortable but not necessarily make a lot of money.

She often complains about her luck with men, and how she always seems to get involved with the "wrong type". Even in a good relationship, she feels a lack of trust and deep intimacy.

Bonnie gets angry when she recalls how her mother treated her as a child. She believes her mother had an unconscious dislike of her ever since she was born, because she competed with her mother for her father's attention. He genuinely loved Bonnie, she feels, but owned a restaurant and seemed to be absent most of the time. In high school, she was moderately popular, yet underneath she felt shy.

Trying hard to be good and do the right thing, Bonnie leads a correct and very proper life. She pays a lot of attention to things of importance to her, such as her job and her membership in volunteer organizations. Sometimes she gets a bit overwhelmed with all the activities she takes on and in her efforts to balance all her commitments.

Bonnie is pleasant and well mannered. At times, she likes to sit back and relax, joke and laugh.

Champions

John was born into a poor family and has eight sisters and brothers. He was the third child of a mild-tempered but overworked mother and an intimidating father. John was the family scapegoat, probably because he could not stand up to his father. When there was punishment to take, John was usually the one who took it.

He never had many friends and didn't much worry about it. After a year of college, he quit and became a police officer. He has had no regrets about that and now at twenty-four, he enjoys his career.

John is very intense and difficult to get to know, but once he is close to someone, he is a true friend. He is a champion of the underdog and a protector of the weak—and also a black belt in karate.

Married, he is fiercely loyal to his family and a tough but very loving father to his achiever children.

Peacemakers

Sam is the youngest of three children and was a bit lost in the shuffle. The members of his family were not particularly close to one another, but they all kept on pretty good terms.

He was shy as an adolescent and had acceptable but not spectacular grades. Sam had a fair number of friends and went on to the state university, where he earned a degree in political science.

Straight from college, Sam went into the family business, which consists of transforming industrial-size rolls of gift wrapping into domestic-use-size rolls and wholesaling them to local retail stores. On his twenty-ninth birthday, his father retired and he took over the business. He's a good administrator and easy to get along with.

Sam has a stable marriage and lives for his family and work. He enjoys spending time with his children. His goals in life are to be a good father, do a good job, and be comfortable.

Helpers

Mary taught school for five years and then married a strong man who could take care of her. She picked a winner. He became a state judge, and she enjoys being the power behind the throne and supporting him. Now forty-six, she has four children, the eldest one in college.

Still in love with her husband after all these years, she keeps her children and his continued career success as her main goals in life. Mary quit her job when her first child was born and only went back to teaching when the kids got older. Now she works with handicapped children.

A good mother who spent a lot of time with her children, she had difficulty letting go of family control and allowing her children to develop into independent persons.

In her childhood, Mary was closer to her father than her mother and was never very close to the only other child in the family, a brother. In high school, she was popular with everyone and had lots of boyfriends. Mary felt sad when she was alone; however, in public she was almost always happy. In spite of her popularity, she was not really a leader. On occasion, she could be aggressive—but always in a sweet way. After graduating from college, she taught at an elementary school and loved it.

Mary has never lost her sense of playfulness and is always willing to make pleasant small talk. While she likes to help others, she has no objection to being the center of attention herself.

Achievers

Scott learned early in life that the way to get attention is to do something. His graduate degree—a master's in business administration—gave him a good start with the sales division of a prestigious manufacturing company. Push and hard work enabled him to climb the corporate ladder.

Nearing retirement age (he's sixty-two), he plans to continue working and not let anyone put him out to pasture.

As a child, he was admired by his father for his ability to accomplish what he set out to do. However, his father did not often express this admiration to his son. In high school, Scott took up bodybuilding and excelled at sports. Both there and later in college, he had good grades, good study habits, and fit in well socially with other students.

He married right after graduation, but it didn't work out. A few years later he married again, and this time found a more suitable partner. He has always put in long hours at work and seldom a great deal of time at home, but this has not been a problem in his second marriage because his wife has her own interests and they have no children.

Although Scott is a charming person, he can be abrupt. He always seems to be in a hurry to get on to the next thing on his list of priorities.

Artists

Patricia had a series of short relationships before getting married and having helper children. Her husband and she have had a stormy life together, with several separations and reconciliations. She is twenty-eight.

In her first jobs, Patricia had difficulties with supervisors who she felt did not understand her. Eventually she found a suitable job and is now a successful commercial artist, known for her sense of design.

As an unplanned baby, she was an inconvenience to her family, and she and her mother seldom got on. Her father died when she was six, and she still feels a special closeness to him. In high school, she was into alternate life-styles. She went on to art school, but dropped out after two years.

Patricia, while very close to her kids, feels it's important that her husband spend time with them too, so that she can have time to herself. She keeps her life interesting, creative, and dramatic. Involved in various political causes, she de-votes most energy to Greenpeace. She also likes to read, go to movies, and travel.

Having stopped going to church while still young, Patricia has recently found God. She still feels she needs to do something unique and individual with her life.

Observers

Tim, now thirty, remembers that his mother had the ability to be both very present in his life and very absent from what was actually happening to him. His father spent much time on the road as a salesman and, when home, he often scared his son, sometimes with his coldness, other times with his anger.

In adolescence, Tim was very shy around girls. He was somewhat of a loner. In college, he gained self-confidence but never had more than a few friends. His grades were reasonably good, and he graduated with an electronic engineering degree.

Tim works as a computer expert for U.S. Customs, and at his location he is the only one who can do what he does. But he never claims that he is indispensable; instead, he quietly and consistently turns in good work without supervision.

After a five-year engagement, he finally got married.

Tim likes to fantasize and daydream. He also reads a lot, and is a collector and tinkerer. One of his collections is of the different kinds of wood that grow in North America. He is happy with his life, and sees no reason why he will not continue to be, as long as he is comfortable and left alone when he desires.

Loyalists

Frank is a thirty-three year old attorney with a successful practice in criminal law. He is happily married to a wife who stays at home to take care of their two kids in the style of the traditional American family. Frank is sweet to his daughter, tough on his son. His many friends find him somewhat aggressive and always antiauthority.

Frank's power struggles with authority began with his father, who was a strict disciplinarian. Frank was close to his mother. His troubles with authority continued through a rough adolescence, and he got into a fair amount of trouble. Then he straightened up and went to college—and continued to argue with his teachers. These days, Frank knows the limits of rebellion and how to play the game.

Although he is afraid of heights—to the point of getting nervous when standing on a ladder more than a few feet above the ground—he has taken pilot lessons and joined a club that is building its own airplane from precut aluminum parts. Frank has volunteered to be its test pilot.

Optimists

Kathy wrote poetry and was the editor of her high school newspaper. After graduating from college, she became a professional journalist and continued to write poetry on die side.

The veteran of a number of relationships, at age thirty-four she is unmarried and unconcerned about it. She has a broad range of interests and is politically active. Her goal is to enjoy life and not suffer.

Because she was the first grandchild on both sides of her family, Kathy was treated like royalty—until her brother was born. She resented the way he diverted from her attention that had always been hers. Popular, she was a member of her high school swimming team.

Today Kathy mixes in many circles, and her separate sets of friends do not always get along together when they en-counter each other through her. So far as Kathy is concerned, however, they are all her friends and fit just fine together.

Personality Types That Can Be Confused

Certain personality types can be confused with others. This occurs because the members of the two groups share some similar characteristics. In many cases, the characteristics are most similar at first glance—and seem less so when looked at more closely.

Since they have the same brain center, any of the personalities of that center could be confused. These are:
- The Instinctive Brain (Gut - Anger) Peacemaker - Champion – Perfectionist
- The Emotional Brain (Heart -Feelings) Achiever - Helper – Artist
- The Logical Brain (Head - Fear) Loyalist - Optimist - Observer

Here are the six likeliest other combinations that can cause confusion, and reliable ways to tell them apart.

Perfectionists and Observers

Observers are more involved in internal control, while Perfectionists care more about outer control, such as over other people and over things. Observers look inward; Perfectionists look outward.

Perfectionists and Loyalists

Loyalists are more concerned with keeping safe, while Perfectionists are involved in making things right. Both have many rules, but Loyalists have safety rules and Perfectionists have rectifying rules. Loyalists are more likely to be rebellious, and Perfectionists are more likely to be neat and tidy.

Helpers and Peacemakers

Helpers have more pride, try harder to be pleasing to others, and more often expect something in return for what they give. Peacemakers are more amiable and friendly, but they also are less likely to make an effort to impress.

Achievers and Optimists

Achievers don't like to spend much time in thought and are more inclined toward action. Optimists are more concerned with keeping the mind stimulated. In addition, Achievers care far more than Optimists about success and status symbols.

Achievers and Champions

Achievers are more concerned with their image. Champions are brassier and not so worried about how others see them. Achievers are smooth and charming; Champions are confrontational.

Artists and Optimists

Artists are more inclined to be emotional, even saddened by personal problems. Optimists are more theoretical and logical that they do not hesitate to tell you what to do for your own good.

Other Identification Difficulties

The vast majority of people who take the tests given in this book quickly discover their personality type. As with any personality test, a small percentage will have difficulty deciding upon or agreeing with the results. There are three main reasons for this:

1. Those who have carried out extensive psychological self-examination can be misidentified. Such people, in taking the tests, should try to respond as they would have before their psychological self-examination.

2. Some people have difficulty being introspective enough to answer the test questions correctly.

3. The tests were designed for normal, emotionally healthy people. Those undergoing emotional disturbance or psychological trauma can be misidentified as to personality type.

Hidden Fears

Some people who made a fortune claim they were not driven by greed for money or power, but by fear of poverty. Our fears are often every bit as strong as our desires and just as irrational.

We hide our ambitions from other people with good reason. So too, with good reason, we hide our fears. When you know a person's secret fear, you may know their greatest weakness.

All of us share feelings of fear about certain things. For example, an out of control car hurtling towards us will scare anyone. But when we talk about hidden fear of something, we mean we have a stronger than normal fear of it. Rather than the presence or absence of fear, we are referring to the amount of fear one feels.

These hidden fears are not full-fledged mental problems that cause disruptions in everyday life. However, these fears do cause what is called avoidance behavior. This means that, to some extent, people with fear do certain things solely to avoid circumstances that arouse the fear in them.

People of each personality type tend to share a characteristic hidden fear. And they also tend to behave in a similar way to avoid arousing this fear. Here's how the different personalities resist their particular fears.

Perfectionist

Perfectionists fear hot, boiling over anger. Instead, they tend to be cold and resentful, leaving their anger unresolved

Champion

Champions fear weakness in themselves. Instead, they become powerful and stand up for themselves and others.

Peacemaker

Peacemakers fear conflict and strife. Instead, they seek harmony and peace at any price.

Helper

Helpers fear having personal needs. Instead, they take care of the needs of others.

Achiever

Achievers fear failure and disgrace. Instead, they get comfort by identifying with success

Artist

Artists fear having average or commonplace lives. Instead, they embellish their lives so that they seem to be unique to others.

Observer

Observers fear lives without meaning and structure. Instead, they fill their empty moments with facts and learning.

Loyalist

Loyalists fear separation or rejection from their families, friends, and coworkers. Instead, they are loyal and careful to avoid disapproval.

Optimist

Optimists fear pain and suffering. Instead, they plan ahead carefully to avoid pain and focus on pleasant things.

Personality Strengths

Who hasn't listened to well-meant advice about getting to know our own weaknesses? We are advised much less often to get to know our own strengths, which is at as least as—if not more—important than getting to know our weaknesses.

By knowing our own weaknesses, we can avoid areas in which we are particularly vulnerable. By knowing our strengths, we can increase our efforts when we recognize ourselves to be in a strong position and thereby maximize our returns. These may be psychic returns, such as affection or tranquility, or physical returns, such as hard cash or good health. This chapter deals more with the psychic returns. It is not about how to get rich or keep fit—at least not directly, although people in good emotional health are most liable to earn high incomes and feel well physically.

Perfectionists

Perfectionists do the right thing. They are not easily influenced by social pressures if these go against what they think is right. Not overly concerned whether others like or dislike what they do, they act according to their own values.

Mature Perfectionists have an aura of emotional calm about them—a kind of tranquility or sense of being at ease with themselves.

Perfectionists are careful and good at tasks that do not necessitate speed. Their sense of humor is liable to be like that of Johnny Carson. And they generally dig in and hold their ground on any matter of principle.

Champions

With Champions, what you see is what you get. Champions really let people know where they stand. They have no problem in confronting life.

They can be loyal, devoted friends. In general, they are not practical jokers or mischievous, and are defenders of the weak.

Beneath their hard outer shell, Champions are gentle and empathetic.

Peacemakers

Peacemakers are good at seeing all sides of an issue. They can make quick decisions. They don't hesitate to call a ball or a strike—and usually they make the right call without thinking much about it.

Peacemakers have big hearts. Fairly generous and easygoing, they are there for others and don't expect anything in return.

Helpers

Helpers are very sensitive to various emotional levels. They know what other people are feeling and recognize what they really want. But theirs is not a case of empathy only—they are willing to take care of others, and are very good at it.

They often have a charming silliness and playfulness in the style of Goldie Hawn.

Helpers know how to impress others. Generally, they know how to get people to like them, although this may not be something they care about one way or the other.

Achievers

Achievers are goal-oriented. They give themselves a job to do or set themselves a mark to attain, and give it one hundred percent of their effort. It hardly needs to be said that they work hard.

They mix well with other people, in just about any group that they care to choose.

Achievers know how to look good. They have an awareness of how they as individuals are seen by other people, and an innate gift of knowing how to present themselves to the world.

Artists

Artists have a highly developed artistic sense. They are likely to have one or more talents in almost any field, for example, acting, painting, singing, and writing.

On the other hand, they are deeply in touch with the pain and sadness of existence.

Artists really know how to make an entrance or exit. They know what dramatic effect is and how to use it. Their sense of style and fashion is keen, and they don't hesitate to express themselves as individuals.

Observers

Observers have a good sense of objectivity. Aware of the value of things, and the limitations of time and money, they use the resources at their disposal efficiently.

They are good conversationalists. And they can be good listeners too. Mostly they do not rock the boat or stir up trouble.

Observers are independent and don't look to others to take care of them. This streak of independence makes them good at solo work and even permits them to operate in isolation.

Loyalists

Loyalists have a long attention span. Their ability to concentrate allows them to undertake things that would drive the rest of us crazy because of the carefulness and precision required. They are good at planning and implementing strategies.

Loyalists are adventuresome and take risks. They can be rebellious in a positive way, by questioning and standing up to authority. They are the ones most likely to confront other people with an opposing point of view.

Optimists

Optimists don't have many personal problems. Generally they are social, easy to get along with, and pleasant—even charming. They can be intellectuals.

Optimists have dreams and visions of what's possible. They are idea people and imaginative brain stormers. Theirs is a positive, upbeat approach to life. Often they have discriminating tastes in food, clothing, and many other areas.

Physical Appearances

The physical appearances of the personality types are not as reliable a guide as the emotional characteristics. Indeed, some people refuse to take them seriously at all. You might keep this in mind if some of the physical descriptions do not fit in well with other personality data about yourself or someone else. And, as always, some people are exceptions to the rule. Additionally, these are descriptions of Americans and apply to varying extents to people from other countries. Perhaps the best use for physical appearances is as an initial indicator, giving you a hint about which of the nine personality types a person belongs in.

Perfectionist

Perfectionists are not overly concerned with their image, but they usually have a neat and well-scrubbed look. Their fingernails are usually well cared for; however, some may bite their nails out of anxiety. Their hair may not be cut in the latest style, but it is clean and groomed.

Often Perfectionists have a self-composed face and bright eyes. There can be a tightness around the mouth and jaws, and the lips may be thin. Because of the rigid way they hold their jaws, their voice can sound strained, as with Barbara Walters and Katharine Hepburn. They are usually thin, only seldom overweight.

Champions

Champions can be on the husky side, either with muscles from working out or with flab from overeating. On top of this, they are liable to wear massive jewelry. It's unnecessary to add that they are not overly concerned about their looks.

Champions are apt to strike people as being overbearing, perhaps even obstinate or angry.

Peacemakers

Some Peacemakers are overweight and some are thin. But often they have a heaviness about them, as if they found life too demanding and were drained of energy.

They like to wear jogging suits and other comfortable outfits, often well worn. At times they pull themselves together and dress up, but mostly they look slightly disheveled in their messy homes. Peacemakers have an inert quality about them and usually impress others as being fairly relaxed and pleasant.

Helpers

Helpers usually have a warm and attractive smile. Some have a problem with being overweight. They dress well and not flashy, generally wearing comfortable clothes of good quality but not always of the latest fashion. They normally pay close attention when you talk to them.

Achievers

Achievers often look much younger than they are. Many have an all-American look and emanate a bright confidence. They can give you a big unwavering smile—but it's cooler than that of Helpers.

Achievers dress well. They dress for success and like to look sharp, without being either stylish or unstylish. However, their jewelry is likely to be in fashion, and their clothes appropriate for the occasion. Although they may have to work at keeping the pounds off, they are usually not overweight.

Artists

Artists often have a sad look, especially in their eyes, which may droop at the outer corners.

They dress anywhere from counterculture to the cutting edge of fashion, enjoying different looks and seeming to make each outfit work for them. Jewelry is popular with Artists, sometimes rather large pieces. They like to set off a solid color outfit with a belt, scarf, or beret in a dramatically different color. The key word is drama. They may even use a short dramatic pause before talking.

Observers

Observers often have a sparkle in their eyes. Sometimes a bit pudgy, they are seldom seriously overweight. They are not worried about how they look and couldn't care less about fashion. Although they may wear the same clothes for two days in a row, you will seldom see them wear anything soiled.

They do not have open and comfortable smiles, and they may have a weak chin, which male Observers are apt to conceal with a beard.

Loyalists

Loyalists sometimes have a protruding chin and may be slightly shabby with badly kept fingernails. In dress, they go for comfort rather than chic, but make an exception when needed for the power look.

Many Loyalists radiate a nervous energy. Their speech patterns can be halting.

Optimists

Optimists smile a lot. This is not an Achiever's radiant, confident smile or a Helper's warm smile. It may have a nervous quality to it, yet be a nice smile all the same. They can be teddy-bearish, but are usually not fat.

They dress fairly well and may have a sense of style. Some who are gourmets can be as selective and fastidious about clothes and food. Optimists may wear a brightly colored scarf or sash for dramatic effect, but are not nearly as likely to do so as Artists.

Chapter Five:
Growth And Wisdom For Each Personality

People tend to automatically respond to a problem in the preferred way of their personality. Thinking about a problem without the filter of your personality can lead to a different and often better solution.

Moving beyond your automatic responses is the way to growth and fulfillment. The following chapters will point you towards the direction of growth for each of the nine basic personalities.

Growth for Perfectionists

Perfectionists tend to fear that their closely controlled cold anger will rage out of control. They fear that being wrong and at fault will make them angry. They must face this fear and move through it before major growth can happen.

Growth Can Occur When Perfectionists Are:
• You are more focused on the enjoyment of life and less concerned with everything being perfect.
• You are more aware of the validity of different peoples' values and less critical of others.
• You are more relaxed and less stern.
• You are more aware of your own self worth and less critical of yourself.
• You are more playful and less serious.

• You are more open to express feelings and less self–contained.
• You are more aware that the world is perfect just as it is and less apt to try to change the world.
• You are more willing to go "one step at a time" and less impatient with life.
• You are more accepting of things as they are and less pretending to be happy.
• You are less concerned with perfection and more interested in what enjoyment you can find in life.
• You are less critical of others and their mistakes, and more aware of the contributions of others.
• You are more aware of your own worth and less critical of yourself.
• You are less impatient with life and more willing to go one step at a time.

The strength of the Perfectionist is their focus and clarity. This focus is fundamentally good, but it can be misdirected when details interfere with seeing the big picture.

Perfectionists should keep in mind that what they perceive as demands from others are really the demands of their own internal judge. They would do well to remember that the world is progressing in divine order just as it is. The world will never be perfect, nor indeed is it desirable for it to be perfect. Life is not perfect but a process of growth, day by day. The experience of living need not be solemn and serious but can be relaxing and fun.

Wisdom For The Perfectionist

Each person views the world through his own perspective, as though each individual wears different colored filtered glasses and therefore, reports seeing different colored objects.

Unfortunately, we almost never remove our personal filters, and consequently maintain a distorted viewpoint of reality. An example of this theory is seen when we look at a tree and note our observation. We might see a large umbrella that provides shade from the sun. Other individuals might see a log to turn into lumber. Still others might see a source of beautiful flowers, tasty nuts or leaves to rake. Birds may consider the tree their home, while termites may consider it their food.

Once we see one thing differently, we then have the ability to begin viewing yet other things differently as well. We will understand that there are different ways to perceive the world. While our five senses give us information, we interpret this information in various ways. We give the meaning to what is there. In the past we have chosen to focus on those things that our conditioned mind dictates. Now we begin to recognize that the reality we see is only a very small part of the actual reality.

We sometimes believe that our thoughts or actions do not measure up to our preconceived idea about successful living. These imagined defects then produce feelings of guilt or sin within us, which in turn can lead to low self-esteem or self-punishing behavior.

Our old thoughts of not being perfect enough or somehow lacking only occur due to our conditioning. In fact, you are the perfect you, but you have the choice to confirm or deny this perfection. Although most of humanity unfortunately denies its perfection, the truth of our being is always within us. It is only necessary to take off the false blinders of our old conditioning in order to recognize our kinship to all creation.

Once we really learn this, we will become free of the world's illusions. Knowing our perfect being will free us from lack and limitations.

Replace dream thoughts of perfection, lack and limitation with reality thoughts of love, unity and abundance. Then we can begin to see particular events in our life from a different perspective. All events hold lessons of life's truth.

When you take life too seriously, the result is usually annoyance, disappointment or anger when things do not go as you desire. This seriousness often creates a bitter and unhappy view of life. Instead, remember the pleasure in life and share in the love and sweetness and lightness that can become your world.

This world with all its serious illusions, thoughts and desires is not the kingdom you were born into. The world's illusions imprison us in a world of false perception. Freedom and salvation come from simply letting go of those illusions and receiving a fuller understand of your greater reality.

The power of your mind is totally beyond full comprehension. Yet perfectionists often impose difficult if not impossible standards upon themself and others. It is as if we are trying to play God and create an imaginary sub-world within reality. The solution is to remember that perfection is in the eye of the beholder and others may not share your idea of perfection.

Belief in guilt and blame are hindrances to our growth. Let us choose to free ourselves from blaming others or ourselves.

When we remember that people are only living up to their present understanding of reality, we can forgive their trespasses because they truly don't know what they are doing. They are living in a hypnotic dream and are really not responsible for the actions they take.

People can't properly judge a course of action based on partial evidence. And if they don't know the truth of their being, they cannot have the complete evidence. Their results may be off, but we must not condemn those who are still in the dark. We should choose compassion and forgive them as others have forgiven us.

If we see others committing an error, let us realize that their belief within their hypnotic world is the real culprit. People can only react according to the level of their understanding of the truth.

If we tear a sheet of paper, the two torn edges become opposites. Where one edge has a hill, the other has a valley. Many people will look at one edge and judge it as different from the other edge. Yet before it was torn both edges were created from the same sheet of paper and were once one.

We constantly judge events and people. We consider things to be good or bad, success or failure, more or less. These are the illusions of the world as seen through a mind that perceives reality as sets of opposites. During our childhood, this concept of opposites was useful to make sense out of the confusing stream of information bombarding our consciousness. However, this view of the world gets in the way of presently understanding reality.

When we look at another person, let's not focus on his outward human appearance. Instead, look beyond, and remember that torn paper. Today choose not to form negative judgments against others. This is also our key for getting along with other people.

Growth for Peacemakers

The strength of the Peacemaker is their clear understanding of both sides of a conflict. However, Peacemakers tend to fear conflict and strong emotions, so they minimize and even deny the very existence of their emotions. They fear that emotional discord will destroy their own personal control. They must face this fear and move through it before major growth can happen.

Growth Can Occur When Peacemakers Are:
• You are more active in the pursuit of life and less withdrawn from life.
• You are more successful in business and life and have less problems setting deadlines and timetables.
• You are more action oriented and less oriented towards procrastination.
• You are more of a self-starter and less dependent on direction from others.
• You see love less as a selfish, private thing, and more as something which binds us all together.
• You are more supportive of friends but less dependent on others.
• You are more aware of what is happening and less daydreaming and escaping.
• You are more fixed on the present reality and less concerned with eventual goals.
• You are more engaged in physical exercise and less lazy.
• You are more conscious of the moment and daydream less.
• You are less concerned with the eventual goal and more fixed on the present reality.
• You are less lazy and exercise more.

Peacemakers can learn to be more flexible and accept change. They can increase their flexibility by learning new ways of expressing their feelings even if this upsets others. They can also work to increase their natural abilities, giving more value to their own self-worth.

Wisdom For The Peacemaker

We sometimes give up too soon, thereby avoiding possible conflict. Certainly much of life is not worth arguing about. But we must not avoid arguing for the really important things in our life. We must be tenacious about anything that affects our freedom and personal growth.

Sometimes we withdraw our attention from life. This may take various forms of escape such as just lying around the house watching television.

These escapes allow us to hide from really looking at our lives. We are concerned about what we might see so we don't look. If we bravely stop escaping and look deeply, we will find a life that is empty. The only way to bring lasting meaning into our life is to fully enter into the experience of life.

Holding on to outdated viewpoints of life limits our ability to realize our higher Self. By removing our old restrictive ideas, we can expand our consciousness to include a more comprehensive understanding of life. What more is the purpose of life than growing from infancy into adulthood and progressively seeing life more fully?

Once we can observe an expanded reality in one area of our life, it becomes easier to see expanded reality in other areas as well. This is because we begin to understand that our preconceived ideas about things are only a small portion of the total picture. We soon understand that we can withhold judgments about initial perceptions and thereby observe a larger reality. This encourages us to continue to awaken from our sleep and to know the truth of life even more fully.

We generally think dreams occur only at night when we are sleeping. In fact, dreams also take place during the day. We actually see things as though viewed through a filter, distorting our perception of reality and limiting our ability to rightly see the world. Reality is much more than what we believe we see or touch in the external world. We would do well to realize that we usually see "through a glass darkly".

Certain thoughts help us recall that we are dreaming instead of being focused in reality. They are there to remind us that there are other ways to understand our experience.

Replace dream thoughts of fear, separation, lack and limitation with reality thoughts of love, unity and abundance.

Growth for Champions

The strength of the Champion is the power that they bring to their fight against injustice. However, their growth depends on using their power for humanity and not with the motive of just increasing their own power.

Champions tend to fear personal weakness and control by others. They fear that revealing what causes them anxiety or pain will allow others to take advantage of them. They must face this fear and move through it before major growth can happen.

Growth Can Occur When Champions Are:

• You are more aware of life in shades of gray and less judgmental and see life less as black or white.
• You are more accepting of life as it is and less trying to make life fair and just.
• You are more tender and vulnerable and less macho and tough.
• You are more powerful and self-restrained in the use of power and less abusive.
• You are more caring for others and less self-centered.
• You are more liked and less feared by other people.
• You are more concerned with family and friends and less concerned with money.
• You are more of a leader of others and more helpful towards others, and less aggressive.
• You are more willing to see other people's point of view and less obsessed with being right.
• You see life less in simple black-and-white terms.

- You try less to make life fair and just and accept it more as it is.
- You are less macho and tough and more tender and vulnerable.
- You have less concern about money and more about family and friends.

Champions can learn to remember not to use their power to control others, but instead realize that others have rights. They can guide others and work in a true spirit of cooperation, openness and love. Champions can learn to be willing to drop or soften their hard outer shell.

Wisdom For The Champion

True strength does not come from facing down others or climbing great mountains. This activity is often a cover-up just to prove to ourselves that we are not weak. True strength comes from having the courage to surrender to your true being and perform the work of love and acceptance.

Ego and pride cause many of the problems in the world. Sometimes we are so proud we think that we do not need others. When we are with others, we sometimes attempt to control everything in the relationship. This is not the way to understand the wisdom of the Universe.

In our everyday life it is easy to believe that we are the masters over everything. We build cities and dam up rivers. But every so often something occurs to remind us that humans have infinitesimal power compared to the unknown universe. It may be an earthquake or a flood, or just the rust and decay of time. But Mother Nature has a way of reminding us that mankind's authority is temporary at best.

Opportunities for positive change come much more frequently than we imagine. There is almost always something we can do to improve our life. Change will occur, and when it does the only sage place we can be is in the house of life.

We can see the beauty and health of the true world. We can right the upside-down, crazy world of our dreams and nightmares. All we need to do is to have faith that everything we need to know will be revealed. But remember, it does take faith. Belief in universal good is required even at those times when our logical mind resists.

It is not necessary to live by physical beauty, strength or mental ability. All that Mother Nature has, we have. This realization brings all that we will ever need. If we put our faith in the power of the infinite good, we will be blessed and healed. We can truly experience heaven on earth.

If we view ourselves as separate from nature, we also feel separate from other humans. When we realize we are a part of nature we view other humans as part of us. This enables us to perceive them differently – on a higher level, and acknowledge our oneness. We realize that getting angry with others is the same as getting angry with ourselves. Loving others is the same as loving our self.

As humans, we believe we were created involuntarily and can be destroyed at any time without our consent. We are like frightened children who hear a ghost story and look everywhere for the imaginary ghost. Like children, we see life as filled with pain and danger and seek help wherever we can find it. But the human help we find is temporary at best, and soon new ghosts frighten us.

Fear means you see yourself as a limited being controlled by unpredictable worldly illusions. But you are much more than a limited mind and body. The infinite force did not create you to forever suffer in fear and limitation. You were created with the free choice to see yourself as much more than your physical being. As your reality expands to more fully understand your true eminence, your fear drops away. The gruesome ghost stories no longer control your reactions.

Growth for Helpers

The strength of the Helper is their skill in relationship with others. However, they can become to overly attached to receiving their identity from others and lose their true self.

Helpers tend to panic over what would happen to them if they no longer solely focused on helping others. They fear that they would lose their identity. They must face this fear and move through it before major growth can happen.

Personal Growth Can Occur When Helpers Are:

• You are more giving of unconditional love and less manipulative.

• You are depending less on others for your self-esteem and more on yourself.

• You have a more simple life.

• You help people less in the expectation of something in return and more in a spirit of altruism.

• You acknowledge more your own needs and are less concerned with the needs of others.

• You are less self-deprecating and more self-accepting.

• You are generating more self-esteem from within and less from others.

• You are living a simpler, less complicated life.

• You are more aware of your own needs and less concerned with the needs of others.

• You are more self-accepting and less self-deprecating.

• You are more aware of flattery used as a method of control and less manipulative of others through flattery.

- You are more giving of support with no strings attached and less concerned with seeking approval.

Helpers should recognize their hidden needs and feelings, especially their negative feelings. They should remember that they do matter, that they are important in themselves and not because of their service to others.

Wisdom For The Helper

So much of our life is spent in trying to please others. Pleasing others up to a point is fine but we often overdo it. This need to please others stems from a deep, yet false, belief that we ourselves are not worthy. Nothing can be further from the truth.

In truth, we are not separate and apart from the whole, but we are part of it and worthy of love.

Our worth and sense of true self comes from the power of our life and not the words of other people. We need just listen to the universal truths and we receive everything.

The path towards freedom and happiness is sometimes obscure, and we will no doubt stumble and fall along the way. We must remember to take care of ourselves as well as we care for other. At times it may seem that our new knowledge is very fragile and easily lost. However, the path does spiral upward. We may think we are right back where we started, but we will remember the truth increasingly and more often. This is our enlightenment, our salvation.

We need not be perfect to teach the truth. We may continue to experience times when we forget our Universal connection. Still, we can teach what we know.

Teaching does not mean inflicting our words on those who don't want to hear. Instead, let us teach by example through our compassionate presence, telling only those who really want to know about the truth.

Let us teach what we would learn better. Remember, though, not to charge blindly ahead, attempting to teach those who cannot yet hear. If our own beliefs are still too new and fragile, they can be shattered by the world's hypnotic reaction.

We must not attempt to tell others that they are wrong in their worldview. They will resist us. Trying to force the truth on others could prevent them from being able to hear it in the future. Instead, we live our life by demonstrating our understanding of the eternal truth. Let the light of our life shine through us.

When others come to us and ask our secret, then share, but only cautiously and with discernment. Few people can immediately conceive our jump to a greater reality. Let's teach the truth, but don't go beyond the ability of the student.

It is impossible to understand infinite life with our finite minds. Sometimes certain events occur repeatedly and we can't understand the reasons. Some people are married and divorced a number of times to the same type of spouse. Others hold a series of similar jobs, which end quickly. These types of events continue to occur until we finally learn the lessons that we are meant to learn from the experience.

Occasionally, seemingly dreadful things happen, and we ask why these things happen to us. We would much prefer only pleasant events to occur. Why do "bad" things happen, and then continue to happen? If everything in life were picture perfect, we would seldom learn anything. The various circumstances we confront during routine living are opportunities to grow and to know reality.

Growth means learning truths necessary to the evolution of our inner selves. The specific events we experience are not as important as the truths that we learn from them. Try to consider all life challenges as opportunities to learn. Whenever faced with difficulties of any kind, be thankful for the opportunity to grow. Don't reject the powerful lessons that we can learn from all life's events, whether positively or negatively perceived.

Growth for Achievers

The strength of Achievers is their hard work and their ability to make things happen. However, Achievers fear the appearance of failure and tend to stretch the truth in order to present themselves as successful. They can grow when they take time from their whirlwind of activities to stop and look at the deceptions they have created in their lives, and replace them with truth and integrity.

Growth Can Occur When Achievers Are:

- You are more trusting of the world to operate efficiently on its own and less concerned with being in control.
- You are more cooperative and less competitive.
- You are more truthful and less boasting.
- You are more cooperative and less vain and concerned about status.
- You are more self-assured and less afraid of failure.
- You are more authentic and less influenced by others.
- You are more focused on enduring values of character and integrity and less of the superficial belief that "if it works, it is truth".
- You are more interested in self-improvement and meditation practices, and less afraid of dealing with shortcomings.
- You are more cooperative with others and less seeking attention or praise.
- You are more satisfied in the present moment and less replacing of personal happiness with long working hours.

Achievers can go beyond the fear of failure by committing themselves to a group or cause they believe is of greater importance than themselves. They can realize that they can't do everything alone, and in fact, others can do some things better. They can remember that the end does not justify the means.

Wisdom For The Achiever

It is Mother Nature's good pleasure to bring us food, health and abundance. That is how humans evolved. However, we must decide to accept this gift and not believe in limitation. We must remember our true being. We must recall that we are not separate and apart from nature, but one with it. Nature did not make concepts such as lack and limitation. Healing occurs when we remember that sickness has no power. The hypnotic trance of everyday life attempts to convince us of the power of lack and limitation, but this is not truth. When we remember this truth, lack and limitation disappears.

A rich man does not affirm that he is not poor. Affirmations made through denial will not work, so make only positive affirmations. Don't affirm that you will get better in the future. Affirm that you are healed now. A total change in consciousness is required. Realization of our true identity with the world that made us is all we need.

Holding on to outdated viewpoints of life limits our ability to realize our higher Self. By removing our old restrictive ideas, we can expand our consciousness to include a more comprehensive understanding of life. What more is the purpose of life than growing from infancy into adulthood and progressively seeing things more fully?

Once we can observe an expanded reality in one area of our life, it becomes easier to see expanded reality in other areas as well. This is because we begin to understand that our preconceived ideas about money power and things are only a small portion of the total picture. We soon understand that we can withhold initial judgments about initial perceptions and thereby observe a larger reality. This encourages us to continue to awaken from our sleep and to know the truth even more fully.

We generally ignore the cycles of change that occur in our lives. An example of changing cycles can be seen in the egg that hatches into a caterpillar. This caterpillar spends this part of its life eating large quantities of plant matter necessary for its growth. The larva's life purpose is to feed upon vegetation and grow. This is like the unconscious portion of man's life during which he consumes elements of the material world.

Eventually the caterpillar spins a cocoon, spending this phase of its life in a pupal case in quiet metamorphose. This is like the quiet time a person spends when they are devoted to contemplating the world of illusion and his place in this world.

Finally, a butterfly emerges from the cocoon. The beautiful butterfly no longer eats plant matter but now visits fragrant flowers and drinks their sweet nectar. This compares to person's growth after they realize their connection with the universe when their existence miraculously changes.

Our body also developed through cycles. It began as a sperm and egg that combined to form a one-cell animal in our mother's womb. Was that really us? Once it was a crying baby. Was that really us? Do we have the same thoughts today? Scientists tell us that each molecule in our body is replaced every few years. Where are we?

As we grow older, we continue to change. Who are we? The only answer is that as part of Mother Nature, we are more than those things.

Let us not be fooled by the rewards of the material world. Fame and millions of dollars in the bank do not bring us any closer to true wisdom than someone who may not even have a bank account. All true and lasting demonstrations of abundance, peace, and happiness are internal, not external. These true riches come from your higher self and have nothing to do with more money, a bigger car or a higher position.

Most people believe that there are two powers, the power of their self and the power of the Universe. The belief in two powers comes from the misperception of a power separate and apart from the one Universe. The belief in two powers presents itself as lack, limitation, sin, separation, sickness and death. These states were not created by the Universe, but dreamed by the mind of man. Our realization of the emptiness we see in the material world is the only way to dissolve this illusion. Awaken and see through it!

The challenges and conflicts of the outer world cannot bring lasting happiness. We may have noticed that the goals set by our old conditioned mind do not bring lasting joy once achieved, only fleeting satisfaction. We then quickly seek a new and more difficult goal to accomplish forgetting that only liberation from illusion brings enduring peace and contentment.

Success comes from being steadfastly committed and not quitting. In today's busy world, so many demands are made upon our time and energies that we often become overwhelmed. We feel that we have no control over our lives. However, we can consciously choose to set aside a few minutes a day to practice our contemplation of life on a regular schedule, and we will then be successful. Everyone who truly wants to know and remember their true identity will be motivated to continue and ultimately succeed.

Let us not be fooled by the rewards of the material world. Studies have proved that millions of dollars in the bank do not bring us any closer to happiness than someone who may not even have a bank account. All true and lasting demonstrations of abundance, peace, and happiness are internal, not external.

Growth for Artists

The strength of the Artist is their ability to appreciate and create beauty. However, the Artist can overdo their search for beauty with bizarre results. They grow when they move toward a more simple and unadorned beauty.

Artists resist the commonplace and ordinary and tend to be dissatisfied with life. They feel reality is boring and fear they will become lost in a humdrum existence. They must face this concern and become more contented with things the way they are before major growth can occur.

Your life is evolving in a healthy way as an Artist when:

• You feel less self-pity and envy of others and realize more the oneness of all life.
• You feel less trapped in your own emotional life and more creative.
• You procrastinate less and act more.
• You are more diligent and hardworking and feel less like sabotaging projects.
• You act more instinctively and think less about feelings.
• You feel less pressure to be special and accept more the way things are.
• You are more assertive and feel less like a victim.
• You think less about your idealized self and more about your real self.

Artists can learn to not take everything so personally and can discipline themselves to accomplish tasks regardless of their ever-changing moods. They can recognize that they are part of humanity and that they are not that unique and different. They can learn to remember that happiness consists of accepting what cannot be changed, and to not struggle with wanting things to be different.

Wisdom For The Artist

We cannot cure lack, limitation and suffering because these is illusions and do not really exist. In today's world, a poor person has much more than the richest person two hundred years ago. All we can do is recognize that the appearance of suffering is not real. The choice between joy and suffering is ours. It's our own dream. We can decide between the extremes!

In truth, there is no lack or limitation to fight against. You don't overcome suffering by overpowering anything, but by remembering that there is no real power in the illusion of suffering. Suffering has only the power of the belief that you give to its appearance. Free yourself from suffering. Simply choose joy instead and the suffering disappears, much like darkness disappears when a light is turned on. With the flip of a switch, the darkness was no longer real.

Holding on to outdated viewpoints of life limits our ability to realize our higher Self. By removing our old restrictive ideas, we can expand our consciousness to include a more comprehensive understanding of life. What more is the purpose of life than growing from infancy into adulthood and progressively seeing things more fully?

Once we can observe an expanded reality in one area of our life, it becomes easier to see expanded reality in other areas as well. This is because we begin to understand that our preconceived ideas about things are only a small portion of the total picture. We soon understand that we can withhold initial judgments about our perceptions and thereby observe a larger reality. This encourages us to continue to awaken from our sleep and to know the truth even more fully.

The hypnotic trance of everyday life attempts to convince us of the power of our total uniqueness from other humans. But this is not truth. These cloudy illusions evaporate once illuminated with truth. Our minor uniqueness becomes insignificant and vanishes in the face of universal truth.

It is not easy to view the lack, limitation and the horrors of the world and actively remember that we are more than this. We do not understand the reason these things happen as they do, but infinite truth has reasons.

Our everyday confused and unsure thinking causes the errors in the way we lead our lives. Examining our place as humans in the ever changing and expanding Universe fixes these errors and allows us to go forward free of future errors.

Past events need not affect our present self. We can break out of historic patterns at any moment we choose.

Barriers to our growth result from our own preconceived emotional limitations, which are rooted in our past and future thoughts. They include our belief that something must change before we can fully be happy.

There is nothing in our past that needs to be overcome. We can forgive anything that happened before. Instead of blaming others, let's look for the hidden gift, the life lesson that can help us better understand our life.

Sitting in a room with drawn curtains in complete darkness, we might become alone and afraid, feeling all the pain and suffering of human existence. But throw open those curtains, and the room is flooded with light. The warm loving light, that has been within us since our birth, is now revealed.

Darkness cannot survive when illuminated by this light. So when light comes, darkness loses its appearance of reality. Darkness does not exist except as the absence of light.

When light enters the room, there is still a shadow that accompanies it. Just as we were afraid of the dark, it's also natural to fear the shadows. Most people spend their lives fighting their shadow selves. Instead, throw open those curtains still wider flooding the room with more of the blinding light of love.

Growth for Observers

The strength of the Observer is their intellect and their ability to organize knowledge. They grow when they move toward involvement with others.

Observers tend to fear what would happen to them if they didn't understand life. They can fear getting immersed in the stuff of life without having detached insights about the underlying meanings. They must face this fear and move through it before major growth can occur.

Your life is evolving in a healthy way as an Observer when:

• You are more willing to share with others and become less stingy.

• You are more involved in real living and less in observing life.

• You are more assertive and less afraid of the use of power.

• You are more relaxed and less intense.

• You have more of a "We can do it" attitude to cooperate with others and are less often a loner.

• You are more willing to share knowledge with others and less grasping for knowledge.

• You are more compassionate with others and less judgmental of emotional, feeling people.

• You are more original in your thinking and less repetition of learned facts or data.

• You are more willing to be openly known as an active player in life and less of a minimal participant in life.

Observers can replace insecure thoughts with a confidence that comes from believing they are knowledgeable enough to live bravely in reality together with the rest of humanity.

Wisdom For The Observer

Opportunities for positive change come much more frequently than we imagine. There is almost always something we can do to improve our life. Change will occur, and when it does the only place we can be is in the house of life.

All who seek the truth of life will find it. We will not fail to know this if we really want it. When we seek the truth of life correctly and more fully, we will receive this knowledge.

The world of form is our classroom to learn the truth. It makes available to us lessons for our growth. Everything can be used as a teacher. Every circumstance can lead us to the truth.

Our greatest purpose in life is to remember our true identity as part of the Universe and listen for clear directions.

We will usually remember our purpose, but occasionally we will also forget. The path to correct understanding is not straight. There are both peaks and valleys in our path. Often we will think we are lost. But we will remember again and again as our overall path is upward. We will gradually remember our purpose more frequently and for longer periods.

Living our lives to fulfill human desires is not our purpose, nor satisfying personal goals of supply or power. Our purpose is not achieving personal gain. Rather, our purpose is to remember our true identity. The infinite Universe is not separate and apart from our identity but part of and within each of us.

This very moment, the experience of peace and joy is available to us. It is not dependent on any other person or human power. From the beginning, our dominion over our peace and joy has existed within us. Over time, we have allowed this control to slowly slip away as we put our trust exclusively in various human powers. However, we can remedy this problem right now. We can choose to receive the perfect peace and joy of our existence this very moment. There is no need to wait.

Fearing that others will take advantage of us is counter-productive to our growth. Closing ourselves off from others to be safe reduces our ability to interrelate and learn.

As humans, we believe we were created involuntarily and can be destroyed at any time without our consent. We are like frightened children who hear a horror story and look everywhere for the imaginary ghost. We see life as filled with danger, and seek help wherever we can. But the human help we find is only temporary at best, and soon new ghosts arise to scare us again.

Fear means we see ourselves as limited being controlled by unpredictable worldly illusions. But we are much more than a limited mind and body.

Evolution created us with the free choice to see ourselves as much more than just physical. As our reality expands to more fully understand our true eminence, fears drop away. The gruesome ghost stories no longer control our reactions.

Growth for Loyalists

The strength of the Loyalist is their ability to hold together the groups and institutions they join. However, Loyalists tend to fear what would happen if their group or friends reject or disapprove of them. They must face this fear and move through it before major growth can occur.

Growth Can Occur When Loyalists Are:
- Trusting themselves more and paying less attention to self-doubt.
- You are more self-assured and less anxious.
- You are more trusting of others and less defensive.
- You are more allowing of feeling and intuiting and less talking or thinking.
- You are more trusting of others and the universe and less concerned about security.
- You are more self-affirming and less worried about what society thinks.
- You are more comfortable with life and less cynical.
- You are more aware of the shades of gray and less thinking in terms of black and white.
- You are more responsible and less indecisive.
- You are more faithful towards the positive progress of life and less self-doubting.

Loyalists can overcome their fear of being different from other members of their group and become more independent. They need the courage to risk doing new things instead of doing the same old things repeatedly.

Wisdom For The Loyalist

Life often seems like we're walking on a minefield and never knowing when a mine will explode. Often we become defensive; because we never know when the next explosion will occur.

When we look to someone or some groups for safety and security, we tend to lose our own identity. We become lost in the temporal needs of others and forget the true source of our good.

When we are in group situations it is often difficult to keep our own identity. It is all too easy to submit to the will of the group or leader

No group can really give us the security we so desperately want. Only our understanding of life's truth has the power to truly keep us safe.

We can forgive and undo our past as if it never occurred. In fact, the past never really did occur, because we saw it through a judgmental filter. We selectively remember events, changing the meaning and coloring the results.

We need not suffer for this false past. Let us cut loose this weighty anchor now. It doesn't matter what sins we think we have committed. Let's forgive ourselves today and let go of our past, which need not control our present.

Suffering did not begin in you, so don't judge yourself. It is not your sin or wrong thinking that has caused your pain. Suffering and error are impersonal, so forgive yourself for everything you imagined you did wrong. Error is just an illusion that disappears when you remember the infinite positive power of life.

We can see the beauty and health of the true world. We can right the upside-down, crazy world of our dreams and nightmares. All we need to do is to have faith that everything we need to know will be revealed. But remember, it does take faith. Belief in universal good is required even at those times when our logical mind resists.

It is not necessary to live by physical beauty, strength or mental ability. All that Mother Nature has, we have. This realization brings all that we will ever need. If we put our faith in the power of the infinite good, we will be blessed and healed. We can truly experience heaven on earth.

Most of humanity does not yet see the truth. They are lost in hypnotic illusions, and this distorted viewpoint often causes wrong action. We cannot pass judgment on those who don't understand. They act according to their current limited understanding of truth. If they knew better they would do better.

Don't allow the actions of others to affect your own choice of action. To remain free, we must forgive those who act without knowledge of the truth. We can effect change in their actions without war and destruction.

Remember the law of forgiveness, compassion and doing unto others as we would have others do unto us. No matter what others appear to be doing, forgive them.

Feelings of loneliness, suffering and depression come from one's sense of separation from truth. Unity with humanity instantly restores peace and happiness. Just as light illuminates the darkness, just as there can be no darkness where there is light, there is no suffering when we realize we are more that just ourselves.

Throughout history people have dedicated their lives to the cause of fighting evil. But what we resist will persist. What we focus on grows in importance. When we go overboard to defend ourselves from fear that we are unsafe, we just create more conflict.

Growth for Optimists

The strength of the Optimist is the joy and happiness they bring to others. However, this joy is often not substantial and grounded enough for others to identify with.

Optimists tend to fear pain and suffering. They develop "monkey mind" and fantasize new plans and stay busy to distract themselves from any frightening, painful thoughts. They must face this fear and move through it before major growth can occur.

Growth Can Occur When Optimists Are:

• You are more focused on sobriety and being aware in the moment and less in pursuit of pleasure.

• You are more engaged in actual work and production and less planning.

• You are more concerned with quality and less with gluttony.

• You are more aware of life as a mix of both joy and pain and less seeing life as just pleasure.

• You are more giving to others and less grasping.

• You are more willing to experience unhappiness and less preoccupied with being happy at any cost.

• You are more willing to just observe and know and less dependent on being with others.

• You are more satisfied with life as it is and less feeling deprived of life's joys.

• You are more willing to wait and work for things and less impulsive.

Optimists should stop running away from painful reality and realize that life contains both pain and pleasure. They should be willing to complete their plans even if that is difficult and painful. They should trust life to be OK as it is and not frequently try to escape life by looking for sweetness and pleasure.

Wisdom For The Optimist

The challenges and conflicts of the illusionary outer world cannot bring lasting happiness. We may have noticed that the goals set by our old conditioned mind do not bring lasting joy once achieved, only fleeting satisfaction. We then quickly seek a new and more difficult goal to accomplish, forgetting that only liberation from illusion brings enduring peace and contentment.

Try to consider all life challenges as opportunities to learn. Whenever faced with difficulties of any kind, be thankful for the opportunity to grow. Don't reject the powerful lessons that we can learn from all life's events, whether positively or negatively perceived.

This very moment, the experience of peace and joy is available to us. It is not dependent on any other person or human power. From the beginning of time, our dominion over our peace and joy has existed within us. Over time, we have allowed this control to slowly slip away as we put our trust exclusively in human power. However, we can remedy this problem right now. We can choose to receive the perfect peace and joy of the universe this very moment. There is no need to wait.

When we experience fear, it means that we see ourselves separately, as body or mind and not as part of evolutionary humanity. Once we remember the larger scope of our true nature, we are no longer afraid.

Our freedom from needless pain and suffering in life depends on our becoming awakened from illusion. Perception is a choice; we can consciously choose to focus on pain and suffering or to focus on joy and happiness. We can transform negative and dysfunctional beliefs into more positive ones that work for us.

It is impossible to understand life with our finite logical mind. Sometimes events occur repeatedly and we can't understand the reasons. Some people are married and divorced a number of times to the same type of spouse. Others hold a series of similar jobs that end quickly. These types of events continue to occur until we finally learn the lessons that we are meant to learn from the experience.

Occasionally, seemly dreadful things happen and we ask why these things happen to us. We would much prefer only pleasant events to occur. Why do "bad" things happen? And why do they continue to happen? If everything in life were picture perfect, we would seldom learn anything about life. The various circumstances we confront during routine living are opportunities to learn to see reality.

About The Author

Alan Fensin began his career in the early days of the American space program. He was a key member of the Apollo rocket design team that successfully put a man on the moon. As an electronic engineer, Alan helped design many of the critical elements used in the electrical system of the Saturn 5 moon-rocket. Returning to school, he earned an advanced degree from Tulane University majoring in Behavior Analysis and became very interested in understanding different personalities.

www.ingramcontent.com/pod-product-compliance
Lightning Source LLC
Chambersburg PA
CBHW060930040426
42445CB00011B/871